United States Government Accountability Office

Report to the Ranking Member, Committee on Homeland Security, House of Representatives

I0411845

September 2014

PERSONNEL SECURITY CLEARANCES

Additional Guidance and Oversight Needed at DHS and DOD to Ensure Consistent Application of Revocation Process

September 2014

GAO Highlights

Highlights of GAO-14-640, a report to the Ranking Member, Committee on Homeland Security, House of Representatives

PERSONNEL SECURITY CLEARANCES

Additional Guidance and Oversight Needed at DHS and DOD to Ensure Consistent Application of Revocation Process

Why GAO Did This Study

Personnel security clearances allow people access to classified information that, through unauthorized disclosure, can cause exceptionally grave damage to U.S. national security. In light of recent events, having a high-quality process to determine whether an individual's eligibility to access classified information should be revoked has become increasingly important. DOD and DHS grant the most clearances in the executive branch, and the Director of National Intelligence is responsible for, among other things, oversight of clearance eligibility determinations.

GAO was asked to evaluate revocation processes at DHS and DOD. GAO evaluated the extent to which the agencies (1) track data on these processes; (2) consistently implement government-wide requirements and exercise oversight over these processes; and (3) determine outcomes for employees whose clearances were revoked. During this review, GAO identified possible inaccuracies in DOD's data on eligible personnel with access to classified information and is also reporting on that issue. GAO analyzed agency revocation data, reviewed executive orders, agency guidance, and documents, and interviewed officials from ODNI, DHS, DOD, and their components.

What GAO Recommends

GAO recommends that DHS, DOD, and the DNI take several actions to improve data quality and oversight related to the personnel security revocation process. DHS, DOD, and ODNI generally agreed with GAO's recommendations.

View GAO-14-640. For more information, contact Brenda S. Farrell at 202-512-3604 or farrellb@gao.gov.

What GAO Found

The Department of Homeland Security (DHS) and the Department of Defense (DOD) both have systems that track varying levels of detail related to revocations of employees' security clearances. DHS's and DOD's data systems could provide data on the number of and reasons for revocations, but they could not provide some data, such as the number of individuals who received a proposal to revoke their eligibility for access to classified information, which means that the total number of employees affected by the revocation process is unknown.

Inconsistent implementation of the requirements in the governing executive orders by DHS, DOD, and some of their components, and limited oversight over the revocation process, have resulted in some employees experiencing different protections and processes than other employees. Specifically, DHS and DOD have implemented the requirements for the revocation process contained in Executive Orders 12968 and 10865 in different ways for different groups of personnel. Although certain differences are permitted or required by the executive orders, GAO found that implementation by some components could potentially be inconsistent with the executive orders in two areas. As a result, some employees may not be provided with certain information upon which a revocation appeal determination is based, and may not be told that they have a right to counsel. These inconsistencies in implementation may be in part because neither DHS nor DOD have evaluated the quality of their processes or developed performance measures to measure quality department-wide. Similarly, the Office of the Director of National Intelligence (ODNI) has only exercised limited oversight by reviewing policies and procedures within some agencies. ODNI has not established any metrics to measure the quality of the process government-wide and has not reviewed revocation processes across the federal government to determine the extent to which policies and procedures should be uniform.

DHS and DOD employees whose clearances were revoked may not have consistent employment outcomes, such as reassignment or termination, because these outcomes are determined by several factors, such as the agency's mission and needs and the manager's discretion. Further, most components could not readily ascertain employment outcomes of individuals with revoked clearances, because these data are not readily available, and communication between personnel security and human capital offices at the departments varies.

GAO's comparison of the total number of DOD employees eligible to access classified information to the total number of DOD employees in fiscal year 2013 suggests that DOD's clearance eligibility totals may be inaccurate. Specifically, GAO found that the number of eligible employees exceeded the total number of employees in five DOD components. DOD officials said this discrepancy could be because DOD's eligibility database is not consistently updated when an employee separates. As a result, the total number of government employees eligible to access classified information that ODNI reports to Congress likely overstates the number of eligible DOD employees. Inaccurate eligibility data hampers DOD's ability to reduce its number of clearance holders to minimize risk and reduce costs to the government.

Contents

Tables

Figures

Abbreviations

CAF	Consolidated Adjudications Facility
DHS	Department of Homeland Security
DMDC	Defense Manpower Data Center
DNI	Director of National Intelligence
DOD	Department of Defense
DOHA	Defense Office of Hearings and Appeals
ISMS	Integrated Security Management System
JPAS	Joint Personnel Adjudication System
ODNI	Office of the Director of National Intelligence
OMB	Office of Management and Budget
OPM	Office of Personnel Management
PSAB	Personnel Security Appeals Board

GAO U.S. GOVERNMENT ACCOUNTABILITY OFFICE

441 G St. N.W.
Washington, DC 20548

September 8, 2014

The Honorable Bennie G. Thompson
Ranking Member
Committee on Homeland Security
House of Representatives

Dear Mr. Thompson:

Personnel security clearances allow government and contractor employees to gain access to classified information that, through unauthorized disclosure, can in some cases cause exceptionally grave damage to U.S. national security. Events—such as the May 2010 disclosure of classified documents to Wikileaks, the June 2013 disclosure of classified documents by a former National Security Agency contractor, and the September 2013 shooting at the Washington Navy Yard— illustrate the danger that can be posed from insider threats, which involve individuals with authorized access to government resources and information. While much attention has been paid to the processes for granting a personnel security clearance,[1] equally important are the processes governing whether individuals who have personnel security clearances should retain their access to classified information. If an individual's circumstances change in a manner that raises security concerns regarding whether he or she should continue to be entrusted with access to classified information, then processes exist to take away, or revoke, an individual's eligibility to access classified information, and for that individual to appeal that decision.

After the September 16, 2013, shooting at the Washington Navy Yard, several reviews were initiated and conducted to assess the security clearance process and facilitate progress in evaluating and improving the quality of that process. For example, in February 2014, the Office of

---

[1]We have conducted a large body of work on issues related to the personnel security clearance process going back over a decade. For more information about GAO's past work on personnel security clearances, please see the list of related GAO products at the end of this report.

Management and Budget[2] (OMB) issued a report that assessed risks inherent in the current security, suitability,[3] and credentialing processes and identified recommended solutions to safeguard personnel and protect sensitive information.[4] In November 2013, the Department of Defense (DOD) issued reports from two reviews addressing gaps or deficiencies in DOD programs, policies, and procedures regarding security at DOD installations and the granting and reviewing of security clearances for DOD employees and contractor personnel.[5] In these reports, both OMB and DOD made recommendations related to improving access to information and reducing the number of clearance holders, among other recommendations.

Further, although the report recommendations have not yet been implemented, all three reports recommended continuous evaluation of employees and contractors who are eligible for access to classified information, which involves automated data checks from sources such as credit checks, social media, and personnel records to provide near-real-time notification of relevant information to help identify potential risks to national security. Implementation of continuous evaluation could prompt further investigation of events and incidents that could lead to an increase in the number of revocations that are proposed by government agencies.[6]

---

[2]Executive Order 13467 appointed the Deputy Director for Management at the Office of Management and Budget (OMB) as the Chair of the Suitability and Security Clearance Performance Accountability Council. Executive Order 13467, *Reforming Processes Related to Suitability for Government Employment, Fitness for Contractor Employees, and Eligibility for Access to Classified National Security Information* (June 30, 2008). This council is responsible for, among other things, ensuring the alignment of security and suitability investigative and adjudicative processes, holding agencies accountable for implementation of these processes, and establishing annual goals and progress metrics on results.

[3]Determinations of suitability for government employment in positions in the competitive service, certain positions in the excepted service, and for career appointment in the Senior Executive Service include consideration of aspects of individuals' character or conduct that may have an effect on the integrity or efficiency of the service.

[4]Office of Management and Budget, *Suitability and Security Processes Review: Report to the President* (February 2014).

[5]Department of Defense, *Internal Review of the Washington Navy Yard Shooting: A Report to the Secretary of Defense* (Nov. 20, 2013); *Security From Within: Independent Review of the Washington Navy Yard Shooting* (November 2013).

[6]For example, a DOD continuous evaluation pilot program found that 3 percent of the cases in the pilot had serious derogatory information that resulted in a revocation or suspension of a security clearance.

In addition, the consistent application of revocation processes across different federal agencies has become increasingly important due to the requirement for clearance reciprocity, where executive-branch agencies are required to accept a background investigation or personnel security clearance determination completed by any authorized investigative or adjudicative agency, subject to certain exceptions.[7]

You asked us to assess the policies and practices associated with the security clearance revocation[8] process at the Department of Homeland Security (DHS) and DOD, the two departments that grant the most personnel security clearances in the executive branch. Specifically, we evaluated the extent to which (1) DHS and DOD track data regarding personnel security clearance revocations, and what these data show; (2) DHS and DOD have consistently implemented government-wide requirements in their revocation processes, and DHS, DOD, and the Director of National Intelligence (DNI) exercise oversight over these processes; and (3) DHS and DOD consistently determine the resulting employment outcomes, such as reassignment or termination, of their military and federal civilian employees whose clearances have been revoked. During the course of our review, when analyzing DOD data to determine the proportion of personnel with clearance eligibility whose clearances were revoked, we identified an issue with the accuracy of DOD's data on the total number of persons eligible for access to classified information, and we are also reporting on this issue.

To evaluate how DHS and DOD track revocation data and what these data show, we analyzed revocation data for military and federal civilian employees from DHS's Office of the Chief Security Officer for fiscal years 2011 to 2013; and for military, federal civilian employees, and contractor personnel government-wide[9] from DOD's Defense Manpower Data Center for fiscal years 2009 to 2013. To assess the reliability of these

---

[7]The Intelligence Reform and Terrorism Prevention Act of 2004, Pub. L. No. 108-458, § 3001 (2004) (codified as amended in relevant part at 50 U.S.C. § 3341).

[8]For purposes of this report, references to revocation of an employee's security clearance means revocation of an employee's eligibility to access classified information.

[9]For purposes of this report, references to contractors government-wide means contractors for DOD or one of the 27 other federal agencies that follow DOD guidance and processes because the Secretary of Defense has entered into agreements for them to adhere to the DOD guidance for their contractor workforces.

data, we reviewed the revocation data and supporting documentation and discussed their reliability with agency officials. We found DHS's and DOD's data on the number of revocations and the reasons for the revocations to be sufficiently reliable for our purposes.

To evaluate the extent to which DHS and DOD have consistently implemented government-wide requirements in their revocation processes and exercise oversight, along with the DNI, over the process, we identified key agency and employee rights and responsibilities in Executive Orders 12968 and 10865[10] and determined whether the agencies were providing employees notice of these rights. We also reviewed applicable federal laws and agency regulations and policies for revoking an employee's or contractor's eligibility for access to classified information, and interviewed personnel security and human capital office officials. We reviewed revocation processes for federal civilian and military personnel within DHS and DOD, excluding the known intelligence community, and for contractor personnel that follow DOD guidance and processes. We also met with DHS, DOD, and Office of the Director of National Intelligence (ODNI) officials to discuss the oversight provided over personnel security revocation processes, their suggestions for building quality into the revocation process, and whether any metrics or reporting requirements exist related to revocations.

To evaluate how DHS and DOD determine the employment outcomes of personnel whose clearances have been revoked, we obtained and analyzed DHS and DOD human capital guidance—specifically their guidance for misconduct, discipline, and adverse actions—and met with human capital office officials to discuss the resulting employment outcomes, such as reassignment or termination, for their military and federal civilian employees. For this objective on managing employment outcomes, within DHS we focused on selected DHS components that had the highest number of security clearance revocations from fiscal years 2011 through 2013: the U.S. Coast Guard, U.S. Immigration and Customs Enforcement, and U.S. Secret Service. Within DOD, we reviewed the headquarters-level elements of the Departments of the Army, the Navy, and the Air Force; the Marine Corps; and Washington Headquarters

---

[10]Executive Order 12968, *Access to Classified Information* (Aug. 2, 1995, as amended); Executive Order 10865, *Safeguarding Classified Information Within Industry* (Feb. 20, 1960, as amended).

Services, which provides human capital support for several nonservice DOD agencies and activities.

During the course of our review, we identified an issue with the accuracy of DOD's data on the total number of persons eligible for access to classified information. To examine the accuracy of DOD's eligibility data, we compared the total number of DOD employees eligible for access to classified information reported by DOD's personnel security management system to the total number of DOD employees in each component. We did not find DOD's data on the total number of current military, federal civilian employees, and contractors who are eligible for access to classified information to be reliable, and our report provides further information on this issue. A more detailed discussion of our scope and methodology is provided in appendix I.

We conducted this performance audit from April 2013 to September 2014 in accordance with generally accepted government auditing standards. Those standards require that we plan and perform the audit to obtain sufficient, appropriate evidence to provide a reasonable basis for our findings and conclusions based on our audit objectives. We believe that the evidence obtained provides a reasonable basis for our findings and conclusions based on our audit objectives.

Background

Roles and Responsibilities of Organizations Involved in Revocation of Personnel Security Clearances at DHS and DOD

Multiple agencies and organizations within DHS and DOD have key roles and responsibilities for different steps of the personnel security clearance revocation process. In 2008, Executive Order 13467 designated the DNI as the Security Executive Agent.[11] As such, the DNI is responsible for developing policies and procedures to help ensure the effective, efficient, and timely completion of background investigations and adjudications relating to determinations of eligibility for access to classified information and eligibility to hold a sensitive position.

---

[11]Executive Order 13467, *Reforming Processes Related to Suitability for Government Employment, Fitness for Contractor Employees, and Eligibility for Access to Classified National Security Information* (June 30, 2008).

Within DHS, the Office of the Chief Security Officer develops, implements, and oversees the department's security policies, programs, and standards, among other things.[12] The DHS Chief of Personnel Security Division, under the direction of the Chief Security Officer, is responsible for issuing department-wide policy for the Personnel Suitability and Security Program, maintaining a departmental database for tracking personnel security cases, and determining employees' eligibility for access to classified information. DHS component Chief Security Officers implement personnel security and suitability programs within their respective component.

Within DOD, the Under Secretary of Defense for Intelligence is responsible for developing, coordinating, and overseeing the implementation of DOD policy, programs, and guidance for personnel security. The DOD Consolidated Adjudications Facility (CAF) determines personnel security eligibility for DOD military and civilian personnel. The DOD CAF was created following a Defense Base Realignment and Closure Commission recommendation to colocate 10 different adjudication activities at Fort Meade, Maryland. In May 2012, the Deputy Secretary of Defense directed the consolidation of the separate functions and resources of seven colocated defense adjudication activities into a single organization. Each of DOD's three military departments—of the Army, the Navy, and the Air Force—has a personnel security appeals board (PSAB) that reviews appeals of cases where a clearance was denied or revoked and makes final eligibility determinations regarding access to classified information for that department's military and civilian employees. In addition, DOD's Washington Headquarters Services has a Clearance Appeal Board, which reviews civilian employee cases for personnel of other DOD components supported by Washington Headquarters Services. The Defense Office of Hearings and Appeals, the largest component of DOD's Defense Legal Services Agency, conducts adjudications, hearings, and appeals and issues decisions in security clearance cases for contractor personnel in the industrial security

---

[12]DHS's current organizational structure includes a headquarters component comprised of directorates and other offices that provide resources, analysis, equipment, research, policy development, and support to its seven operational components: the Federal Emergency Management Agency; Transportation Security Administration; U.S. Citizenship and Immigration Services; U.S Coast Guard; U.S. Customs and Border Protection; U.S. Immigration and Customs Enforcement; and U.S. Secret Service.

program,[13] including DOD and DHS contractor personnel. The Defense Office of Hearings and Appeals also conducts hearings, referred to as personal appearances, and issues recommended decisions in security clearance cases for DOD military personnel and civilian employees. In addition, the Defense Office of Hearings and Appeals has a Security Appeals Board, which reviews appeals of cases where a contractor's personnel security clearance was denied or revoked.

Guidance Governing Revocation of Personnel Security Clearances at DHS and DOD

The overall process for revoking an employee's security clearance is primarily established in two executive orders: Executive Order 12968, which is applicable to all military or federal civilian employees and contractor personnel,[14] and Executive Order 10865, which provides additional rights only to contractor personnel.[15] These executive orders establish two parallel processes for revoking eligibility for access to classified information, with one process applicable to military and civilian employees and a different process applicable to contractors. Figure 1 summarizes the agency's responsibilities and the rights that must be provided to employees who are subject to a security clearance revocation in accordance with these two executive orders.

---

[13]The National Industrial Security Program was established by Executive Order 12829 to safeguard classified information that is released outside of federal agencies, for example, to contractors. Executive Order 12829, *National Industrial Security Program* (Jan. 6, 1993). The Secretary of Defense has entered into agreements with 27 departments and agencies for the purpose of rendering industrial security services. One such industrial security service is provided by the Defense Office of Hearings and Appeals, which provides adjudications, hearings, and appeals of security clearance cases for private-sector employees (contractors) working in the National Industrial Security Program.

[14]Executive Order 12968, *Access to Classified Information* (Aug. 2, 1995, as amended).

[15]Executive Order 10865, *Safeguarding Classified Information Within Industry* (Feb. 20, 1960, as amended).

Figure 1: Personnel Security Clearance Revocation Rights and Responsibilities Provided by Executive Orders

Executive Order 12968: Civilian, Military, and Contractor Personnel

Agency Responsibilities

Agencies must provide employee with the following:
- Written explanation for basis of revocation action, as detailed as permitted by national security interests and applicable law
- Any documents upon which revocation is based within 30 days of request, to the extent that documents would be provided under the Freedom of Information Act or Privacy Act
- Written notice of and reasons for results of review
- Identity of deciding authority
- Written notice of right to appeal
- Final written decision by appeal panel

In addition, if the employee chooses a personal appearance, the agency must make a written summary or recording of the personal appearance part of the employee's security record.

Employee Rights

Employees have the following rights in the process:
- Representation by counsel at employee's expense
- Request any documents on which revocation is based, and entire investigative file, as permitted by national security and other applicable law
- Reply in writing to determination
- Request review of determination
- Opportunity to appeal in writing to three member high level appeal panel
- Request a personal appearance before adjudicative authority

Executive Order 10865: Contractor Personnel

Agency Responsibilities

In addition to the responsibilities listed in Executive Order 12968, agencies must provide employee with the following:
- Reasonable time to prepare for personal appearance

Employee Rights

In addition to the rights listed in Executive Order 12968, employees are entitled to the following rights:
- Reply in writing to determination under oath or affirmation
- Opportunity to cross-examine persons who have made adverse oral or written statements relating to a controverted issue, subject to certain exceptions

Source: GAO analysis of Executive Orders 12968 and 10865. | GAO-14-640

DHS and DOD also provide supplemental guidance and clarification regarding the revocation process to their respective components. DHS Headquarters and its components follow DHS Instruction Handbook 121-01-007,[16] and some DHS components have additional guidance.[17] DOD

---

[16]DHS Instruction Handbook 121-01-007, *The Department of Homeland Security Personnel Suitability and Security Program* (June 2009), Chapter 6.

[17]For example, see U.S. Customs and Border Protection, Office of Internal Affairs, Personnel Security Division, HB1400-07A, *Personnel Security Handbook* (August 2011); U.S. Secret Service, *Human Resources and Training Manual, Section RPS-02 (02): Suspension, Denial, or Revocation of Access to Classified Information—Interim Procedures* (May 30, 2003); U.S. Coast Guard COMDTINST M5520.12C, *Personnel Security and Suitability Program* (Mar. 18, 2010).

and its components follow DOD Regulation 5200.2-R.[18] DOD contractors are subject to the personnel security policies and procedures in DOD Directive 5220.6,[19] and related DOD guidance for contractors to safeguard classified information under the National Industrial Security Program.[20] The Secretary of Defense has entered into agreements with 27 other federal agencies, including DHS, to adhere to the DOD guidance for their contractor workforces. Furthermore, the military departments and Washington Headquarters Services provide supplementary guidance and clarification of the revocation appeal process found in the DOD regulation.[21] According to officials from the Defense Office of Hearings and Appeals, by mutual agreement, 23 other federal agencies, including DHS, use the Defense Office of Hearings and Appeals for adjudications, hearings, and appeals of security clearance revocation cases for contractors working in the National Industrial Security Program.

---

[18]DOD Regulation 5200.2-R, *Personnel Security Program* (January 1987, incorporating administrative change Feb. 23, 1996). This regulation is being revised, and DOD officials stated that it will be replaced by a two-volume DOD manual, which is currently in draft. The DOD directive that this regulation had implemented has recently been reissued as a DOD instruction. See DOD Instruction 5200.02, *DOD Personnel Security Program* (Mar. 21, 2014), cancelling DOD Directive 5200.2, *DOD Personnel Security Program* (Apr. 9, 1999).

[19]DOD Directive 5220.6, *Defense Industrial Personnel Security Clearance Review Program* (Jan. 2, 1992, incorporating administrative change Apr. 20, 1999) as modified by Undersecretary of Defense for Intelligence Memorandum, *Implementation of Adjudicative Guidelines for Determining Eligibility For Access to Classified Information* (Aug. 30, 2006).

[20]DOD Manual 5220.22-M, *National Industrial Security Program Operating Manual* (Feb. 28, 2006, incorporating change Mar. 28, 2013).

[21]Army Regulation 380-67, *Personnel Security Program* (Aug. 4, 2011); Secretary of the Navy Manual M-5510.30, *Department of the Navy Personnel Security Program* (June 2006); Air Force Instruction 31-501, *Personnel Security Program Management* (Jan. 27, 2005, incorporating through change 2, Nov. 29, 2012); Washington Headquarters Services Administrative Instruction 23, *Personnel Security Program and Civilian Personnel Suitability Investigation Program* (Dec. 20, 2006).

| Personnel Security Clearance Revocation Process | DHS and DOD can revoke an employee's eligibility for access to classified information based on 13 adjudicative guidelines.[22] While the personnel security clearance revocation process varies by agency and type of employee, the general process for DHS and DOD military and federal civilian personnel, and for government contractors, is summarized in figure 2. According to DHS officials, the revocation process will end if the employee chooses to resign before a decision has been made; if a DOD military or civilian employee has initiated an appeal of a revocation decision, the appeal will be decided even if an employee has separated.[23] |

---

[22]The adjudicative guidelines base security clearance decisions upon consideration of the following 13 areas: allegiance to the United States; foreign influence; foreign preference; sexual behavior; personal conduct; financial considerations; alcohol consumption; drug involvement; psychological conditions; criminal conduct; handling protected information; outside activities; and use of information technology systems.

[23]If an employee resigns after a revocation has been proposed but prior to a revocation decision, DOD officials said that for contractors and DOD personnel, the DOD personnel security clearance database should show an eligibility status called "Loss of Jurisdiction." Such designation would notify other agencies that the employee has undetermined status for access to classified information, according to ODNI officials. DHS officials said that DHS's personnel security clearance database would change the eligibility status of an employee if the employee's clearance was suspended prior to a revocation decision. If the clearance was not suspended prior to a revocation decision, then there would not be a change in eligibility in the DHS database that would notify other agencies that a DHS employee may have an unresolved issue unless a DHS security specialist manually inserts a message such as "please call."

Figure 2: Typical Processes to Revoke DHS, DOD, and Contractor Personnel Security Clearances

		 Adverse information received	Proposal to revoke clearance	Decision to revoke clearance	 Appeal of revocation decision
	**Department of Homeland Security** *Military and civilian personnel*	**Component or headquarters personnel security office** • Receives and reviews adverse information	**Component or headquarters personnel security office** • Issues proposal to revoke clearance to employee Employee has 30 days to respond and refute, clarify, or explain the adverse information	**Component personnel security office official or headquarters Chief of Personnel Security Division** • Reviews case file • Issues decision Employee has 15 days to request documentation used in making decision and 30 days to appeal after receiving documentation; or 30 days to appeal if no documentation requested; decision becomes final if not appealed	» **Initial Appeal: Supervisory personnel security official, Chief Security Officer, or designee** • Reviews case file and additional information provided by employee in writing or during personal appearance • Issues decision Employee has 15 days to appeal and 30 days to provide information to appeals board » **Final Appeal: Security Appeals Board** • Reviews case file and any additional written information provided by employee • Issues final decision
	**Department of Defense** *Military and civilian personnel*	**Consolidated Adjudication Facility (CAF) adjudicator** • Receives and reviews adverse information	**CAF adjudicator** • Issues proposal to revoke clearance to employee Employee has 30 days to respond and refute, clarify, or explain the adverse information	**CAF adjudicator** • Reviews employee's response • Issues decision Employee has 10 days to indicate intent to appeal either in person or in writing; decision becomes final if not appealed	**Defense Office of Hearings and Appeals (DOHA) Administrative Judge** • Presides over personal appearance if employee chooses in-person appeal • Submits nonbinding recommendation to relevant service Personnel Security Appeals Board (PSAB) **PSAB** • Written appeals: reviews case file and new information provided by employee • Appeals with personal appearance: reviews the administrative judge's recommendation and case file • Issues final decision
	Contractors	**CAF adjudicator** • Receives and reviews adverse information	**CAF adjudicator** • Issues proposal to revoke clearance to contractor Employee has 20 days to respond and refute, clarify, or explain the adverse information	**DOHA Administrative Judge** • Reviews case file and additional information • Presides over personal appearance, if employee chooses to have a personal appearance • Issues decision Employee has 15 days to appeal the decision; decision becomes final if not appealed	**DOHA Appeal Board** • Reviews case file and appeal brief • Issues final decision

Source: GAO analysis of DHS and DOD information. | GAO-14-640

GAO-14-640 Security Clearance Revocations

The process begins with adverse information that can come from a variety of sources, including but not limited to individual self-reporting, federal or contract investigators who are conducting an investigation, Inspector General channels, hotlines, civilian law enforcement agencies, and reporting by persons such as security officers. According to DHS and DOD officials, the steps and time frames associated with investigating and verifying the credibility of the adverse information can vary considerably according to the nature and source of the adverse information. Some of these steps may include notifying the employee that adverse information was reported against him or her, allowing the employee an opportunity to provide a response, obtaining information from other government agencies, and conducting an updated background investigation to obtain court records, criminal records, and financial checks.

The February 2014 OMB report found that clear and consistent requirements do not exist across government for employees or contractors to report information that could affect their continued fitness, suitability, or eligibility for federal employment and that there was not consistent guidance in place to direct contractors or contract managers to report noteworthy or derogatory information regarding employees.[24] The report recommended acceleration of the implementation of a continuous evaluation program that would notify security officials of noteworthy events or incidents in near-real time. If incident reporting increases as a result of these recommendations, it raises the potential that such incidents could lead to an increase in the number of revocation cases in the future. As part of an ongoing review on the quality of the personnel security background investigation process, we are examining the implementation status of the recommendations in this OMB report.

---

[24]Office of Management and Budget, *Suitability and Security Processes Review: Report to the President* (February 2014).

DHS and DOD Data Systems Do Not Track Complete Revocation Information

DHS's and DOD's data systems track varying levels of detail related to personnel security clearance revocations. DHS's and DOD's data systems could provide data on the number of and reasons for revocations, but they could not provide some data, such as the number of individuals who received a proposal to revoke their eligibility for access to classified information, which means that the total number of employees affected by the revocation process is unknown.

DHS Revoked Clearances of Fewer than 1 Percent of Employees Eligible to Access Classified Information, but It Is Believed That Many Employees Resign before Final Determination Is Made

DHS data show that about 125,000 DHS civilian and military employees were eligible to access classified information as of March 2014, and that DHS revoked access to classified information for 113 employees, or less than 1 percent, in fiscal year 2013. An official from the DHS Office of General Counsel explained that many employees resign before the final determination is made to revoke their security clearance. Importantly, the total population affected by the revocation process is unknown because the number of individuals who received a proposal to revoke their eligibility for access to classified information is unknown, as discussed below. Table 1 shows the number of DHS employees eligible to access classified information as of March 2014, and the number of personnel security clearance revocations for each DHS component in fiscal year 2013, with the U.S. Coast Guard having the largest number of revocations. Coast Guard officials stated that the increase in the number of revocations for Coast Guard military personnel in fiscal year 2013 could be explained in part because that was the first year the Coast Guard enforced the use of position sensitivity codes.[25] They said that, as a result, some administratively withdrawn clearances were counted as revoked, which artificially inflated the revocation number.[26]

---

[25]Position sensitivity codes determine what type of security investigation is required and how closely an individual is screened for a position. These codes are determined by the position designation, which is an overall assessment that involves consideration of the position's duties and responsibilities as they affect specific programs, national security interests, and operations within the Coast Guard.

[26]Coast Guard officials explained that they did not have an accurate way of counting which clearances were administratively removed versus which were revoked for cause without doing a manual review of all of the revocation cases. They stated that a Coast Guard trend analysis supported that the number of revocations for cause in fiscal year 2013 was similar to the number of revocations in fiscal years 2011 and 2012.

Table 1: Department of Homeland Security (DHS) Employees Eligible to Access Classified Information and Personnel Security Clearance Revocations by Component

DHS component	Employees eligible to access classified information as of March 2014	Percentage of total DHS employees eligible to access classified information	Revocations in fiscal year 2013	Percentage of total DHS revocations
U.S. Coast Guard—military	49,614	39.63%	75	66.37%
Transportation Security Administration	20,234	16.16	1	0.88
U.S. Immigration and Customs Enforcement	15,106	12.07	4	3.54
U.S. Customs and Border Protection	12,699	10.14	3	2.65
DHS Headquarters	10,005	7.99	10	8.85
U.S. Secret Service	6,428	5.13	9	7.96
U.S. Citizenship and Immigration Services	5,479	4.38	6	5.31
U.S. Coast Guard—civilian	2,859	2.28	0	0.00
Federal Emergency Management Agency	2,768	2.21	5	4.42
Total	**125,192**	**100.00%**	**113**	**100.00%**

Source: GAO analysis of data from DHS Office of the Chief Security Officer, Personnel Security Division. | GAO-14-640

Note: These data were provided by DHS's Office of the Chief Security Officer using the Integrated Security Management System (ISMS), the DHS system for managing and standardizing personnel security data.

Table 2 provides additional information on the number of personnel security clearance revocations for each DHS component in fiscal years 2011 through 2013.

Table 2: Department of Homeland Security (DHS) Personnel Security Clearance Revocations by Component, Fiscal Years 2011 through 2013

DHS Component	Fiscal Year 2011	Fiscal Year 2012	Fiscal Year 2013	Total
U.S. Coast Guard—military personnel	33	27	75	135
U.S. Coast Guard—civilian personnel	0	5	0	5
Transportation Security Administration	5	6	1	12
U.S. Immigration and Customs Enforcement	12	14	4	30
U.S. Customs and Border Protection	0	3	3	6
DHS Headquarters	3	5	10	18
U.S. Secret Service	9	13	9	31
U.S. Citizenship and Immigration Services	1	4	6	11
Federal Emergency Management Agency	1	0	5	6
Total	**64**	**77**	**113**	**254**

Source: GAO analysis of data from DHS Office of the Chief Security Officer, Personnel Security Division. | GAO-14-640

DHS data show that personal conduct, financial considerations, and criminal conduct were the most common reasons personnel security clearances were revoked in fiscal year 2013. Figure 3 provides details about the issues underlying personnel security clearance revocations for each DHS component in fiscal year 2013.

Figure 3: Reasons for Department of Homeland Security (DHS) Personnel Security Clearance Revocations in Fiscal Year 2013

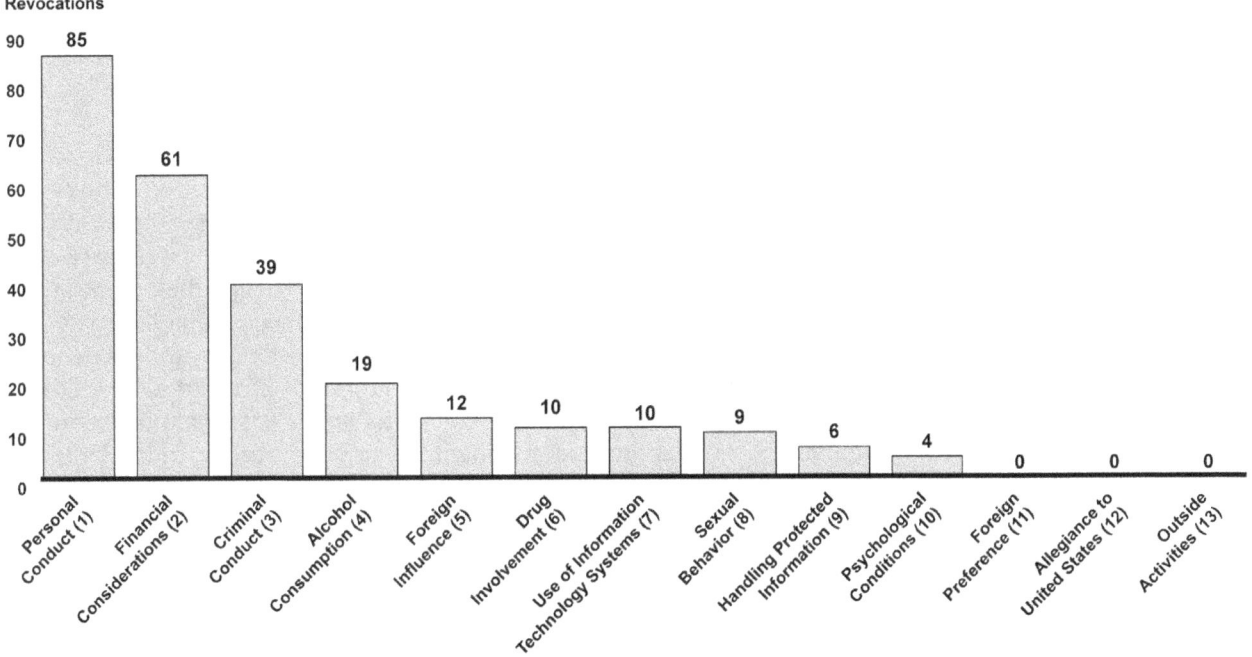

Component	Reasons for security clearance revocation												
	1	2	3	4	5	6	7	8	9	10	11	12	13
U.S. Customs and Border Protection	1	1	1	0	0	1	1	0	0	0	0	0	0
DHS Headquarters	7	0	3	0	0	2	2	1	1	0	0	0	0
U.S. Immigration and Customs Enforcement	5	1	3	0	2	0	3	2	2	0	0	0	0
Federal Emergency Management Agency	5	1	3	0	0	0	0	0	0	0	0	0	0
U.S. Coast Guard	54	53	23	17	9	7	2	4	2	2	0	0	0
U.S. Citizenship and Immigration Services	4	2	1	2	0	0	2	0	1	0	0	0	0
U.S. Secret Service	9	3	5	0	1	0	0	2	0	2	0	0	0

Source: GAO analysis of Department of Homeland Security (DHS) Office of the Chief Security Officer, Personnel Security Division data. | GAO-14-640

Note: Revocation cases may involve more than one reason; therefore, there are more reasons cited in this figure than the total number of revocation cases in fiscal year 2013. DHS provided us with data about the revocation reasons at the Transportation Security Administration; however, because that component only had one clearance revocation case in fiscal year 2013, we are not reporting those reasons due to privacy concerns.

DHS employees whose access to classified information was revoked can first appeal the adverse decision with an initial appeal to a second-level deciding authority, and then appeal this decision with a final appeal to a three-person Security Appeals Board. DHS data show that, in fiscal year 2013, 24 employees appealed a revocation decision to the DHS Security Appeals Board. Of those 24 employees, 1 had his or her security clearance reinstated.

DOD Revoked Clearances of More than 16,000 Employees and 2,500 Contractors from Fiscal Years 2009 through 2013

DOD data show that DOD revoked eligibility for access to classified information for more than 16,000 military and civilian employees from fiscal years 2009 through 2013, and for almost 2,500 contractors government-wide during this same period. Because of potential inaccuracies in DOD eligibility data, which are discussed below, we were unable to determine the percentage of DOD clearance holders whose clearances were revoked. However, as we found with DHS, the total population affected by the revocation process is unknown because the number of individuals who received a proposal to revoke their eligibility for access to classified information is unknown, as discussed in the next subsection in this report. Table 3 shows the number of personnel security clearance revocations in fiscal years 2009 through 2013 for each DOD component, with Army military personnel having the largest number of revocations, and for contractors government-wide working in the industrial security program.

Table 3: DOD and Contractor Personnel Security Clearance Revocations by Component, Fiscal Years 2009 through 2013

DOD Component	Fiscal Year 2009	Fiscal Year 2010	Fiscal Year 2011	Fiscal Year 2012	Fiscal Year 2013	Total
Air Force military personnel[a]	315	317	249	238	192	1,311
Air Force civilian personnel	81	86	59	79	68	373
Army military personnel[a]	354	1,177	2,338	3,092	2,342	9,303
Army civilian personnel	104	140	236	210	218	908
Marine Corps military personnel[a]	225	244	360	329	333	1,491
Marine Corps civilian personnel	1	0	1	2	0	4
Navy military personnel[a]	423	354	354	379	297	1,807
Navy civilian personnel	148	124	139	160	105	676
Washington Headquarters Services civilian personnel[b]	42	43	34	30	44	193
Other[c]	26	16	19	11	8	80
DOD Total	**1,719**	**2,501**	**3,789**	**4,530**	**3,607**	**16,146**
Industry	529	415	498	528	529	2,499
Total	**2,248**	**2,916**	**4,287**	**5,058**	**4,136**	**18,645**

Source: GAO analysis of data from the Defense Manpower Data Center. | GAO-14-640

[a]Military personnel data include counts for active-duty and all reserve categories (Ready Reserve, Standby Reserve, and Retired Reserve), including the National Guard.

[b]Washington Headquarters Services civilian personnel includes personnel employed by other defense agencies supported by Washington Headquarters Services.

[c]The "Other" category includes persons who were assigned to a service in the Joint Personnel Adjudication System (JPAS) (e.g., Air Force, Army, Marine Corps, Navy), but were not assigned to a category type such as civilian, military, or reserves. Defense Manpower Data Center (DMDC) officials stated that these persons would be personnel such as presidential appointees, congressional staff, or Red Cross employees.

The most common reasons for revoking a personnel security clearance for DOD civilian and military personnel in fiscal year 2013 were criminal conduct, drug involvement, and personal conduct. The most common reasons for revocation of security clearances for contractor personnel in fiscal year 2013 were financial considerations, personal conduct, and criminal conduct. Figure 4 provides details about the issues underlying personnel security clearance revocations for each DOD component and for contractors in fiscal year 2013.

Figure 4: Reasons for DOD Employee and Contractor Personnel Security Clearance Revocations in Fiscal Year 2013

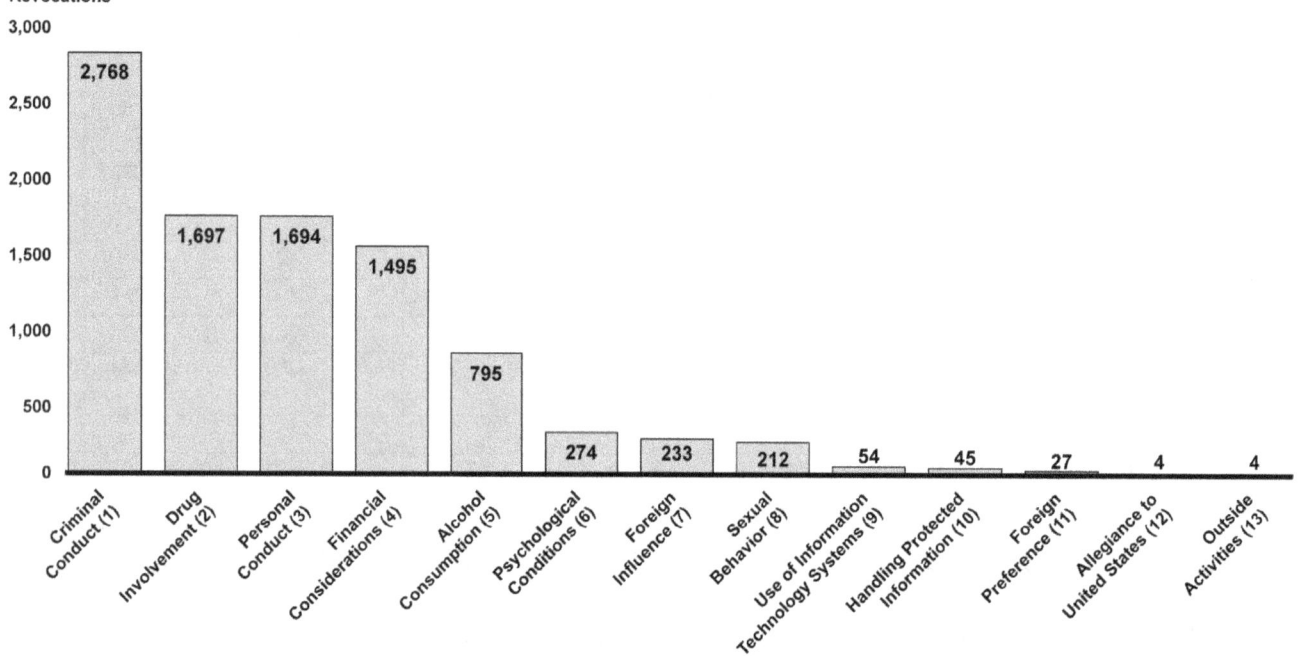

Component	Reasons for security clearance revocation												
	1	2	3	4	5	6	7	8	9	10	11	12	13
Army civilian personnel	119	41	108	138	45	15	17	16	6	2	2	0	1
Army military personnel	1,842	1,118	1,102	750	517	151	86	131	12	14	7	2	0
Air Force civilian personnel	28	8	41	49	14	6	11	5	2	3	1	1	1
Air Force military personnel	94	25	117	147	34	17	35	7	5	1	4	1	1
Navy civilian personnel	70	44	48	67	34	15	12	7	7	9	0	0	0
Navy military personnel	242	161	102	149	59	38	34	22	7	6	6	0	0
Marine Corps military personnel	305	262	83	83	64	21	11	14	4	3	3	0	0
WHS civilian personnel	13	7	20	28	2	5	7	1	4	1	1	0	0
Other	7	6	4	4	0	1	2	0	1	0	1	0	0
Industry	48	25	69	80	26	5	18	9	6	6	2	0	1

WHS: Washington Headquarters Services
Source: GAO analysis of Defense Manpower Data Center data. | GAO-14-640

Note: Revocation cases may involve more than one reason; therefore, there are more reasons cited in this figure than the total number of revocation cases in fiscal year 2013.

DHS's and DOD's Systems Do Not Capture All Revocation-Related Data, Including the Total Population Affected by the Revocation Process

Although DHS's and DOD's data systems could provide data on the number of and reasons for revocations, neither department is currently required to track or report security clearance revocations data or any related metrics outside of the DHS and DOD elements of the intelligence community.[27] As a result, neither system could provide data on how many individuals separated before a revocation decision was made, appeals, and time to complete a revocation case. Notably, neither the DHS nor the DOD system was able to provide data about the total number of individuals who received a proposal to revoke their security clearance, which would likely exceed the total number of revocations. Therefore, we are unable to comment on the total number of employees who might be affected by the revocation process. In order for organizations to measure performance, it is important that they have sufficiently complete, accurate, and consistent data to document performance and support decision making, while balancing the cost and effort involved in gathering and analyzing data.[28] DHS's system for managing and standardizing personnel security data, the Integrated Security Management System (ISMS), has not typically been used to track additional information about security clearance revocations, such as (1) the number of employees who received a proposal to revoke their clearance, (2) the number of employees who separated from the department before a revocation decision was made, (3) the number of employees that filed an initial appeal of a revocation decision, and (4) the length of time to complete a revocation case.

First, DHS officials could not provide us with data on the number of individuals who had received a proposal to revoke their clearance. They said that this information could be recorded in ISMS, but that this capability may not be used by all of the components. Second, DHS

---

[27] The Intelligence Authorization Act for Fiscal Year 2010, Pub. L. No. 111-259, § 367 (2010) (codified in relevant part at 50 U.S.C. § 3104), established a requirement that the President annually report to Congress the percentage of reviews during the preceding fiscal year that resulted in a denial or revocation of a security clearance for each element of the intelligence community. However, this reporting requirement does not apply to executive-branch agencies outside of the intelligence community, such as the nonintelligence components within DOD and DHS. Our review excluded known intelligence community military and civilian personnel and contractors.

[28] GAO, *Assessing the Reliability of Computer-Processed Data*, GAO-09-680G (Washington, D.C.: July 2009), and *Executive Guide: Effectively Implementing the Government Performance and Results Act*, GAO/GGD-96-118 (Washington, D.C.: June 1996), pp. 24, 27.

officials said that ISMS does not track cases where an individual separated from the department before a decision was made regarding a proposal to revoke a personnel security clearance. For example, DHS officials said that if an employee was issued a proposal to revoke his or her clearance and he or she resigned and never responded to the proposal, then the security clearance was never revoked and the case would not be counted as a revocation. Once an initial decision is made to revoke a clearance, the decision is entered into ISMS and that decision will become final even if the employee does not respond, so those cases would be counted. Third, DHS data on the number of employees that filed an initial appeal of a revocation decision were not available. Officials from the Office of the Chief Security Officer told us that ISMS has a module that could provide this information, but because use of this module is not required, only a few DHS components use it. Finally, while officials at DHS components stated that the entire revocation process can take over a year to complete, DHS data on the average amount of time it takes to complete a revocation case were not available. Officials from the Office of the Chief Security Officer said that while ISMS can identify this information in individual records, it cannot track this type of data as a whole across the DHS components, because each appeal level would be saved as a different module entry. They said they try to complete a revocation case as quickly as possible. However, in some cases, employees request extensions of time in order to obtain representation or to obtain documents to refute or explain the revocation decision, which lengthens the process time. Until DHS considers whether tracking additional revocation and appeals information would be beneficial, and modifies its system to provide such information as is deemed beneficial, the department will continue to lack visibility over certain aspects of the security clearance revocation and appeal process, which may hinder its ability to effectively oversee these processes.

Similarly, DOD's Joint Personnel Adjudication System (JPAS) system, which is designated as DOD's system of record for personnel security management to record and document personnel security actions, [29] also captures varying levels of detail related to security clearance revocations.

---

[29]JPAS is used by the military departments, defense agencies, and industry to manage employee eligibility for access to classified information and is managed by the Defense Manpower Data Center (DMDC). DMDC is a component of the DOD Human Resources Activity, which is under the authority, direction, and control of the Under Secretary of Defense for Personnel and Readiness.

GAO-14-640 Security Clearance Revocations

We found certain JPAS data fields partially completed or incomplete, such as fields showing whether an employee received a proposal to revoke his or her clearance, whether the employee chose to appeal the revocation decision in writing or in person, the time taken at different stages of the employee's revocation appeal, and the number of employees who separated from the department before a revocation decision was made. For example, although more than 16,000 military and federal civilian employees had their personnel security clearances revoked from fiscal years 2009 through 2013, JPAS data reflected that fewer than 3,000 individuals had received a statement of reasons, which is DOD's initial proposal to revoke a personnel security clearance, because the JPAS field to record this information had not been filled.

The JPAS system of record notice, dated May 3, 2011, states that the categories of records in JPAS include records documenting the personnel security adjudicative and management process.[30] However, officials from the Defense Manpower Data Center (DMDC), DOD's JPAS administrator, and the DOD CAF stated that DOD users instead generally used component-specific case-management systems to keep track of adjudication information.[31] DMDC officials explained that the final eligibility determination, and not all the other adjudication data, from the different case-management systems was uploaded to JPAS. Officials from the Office of the Under Secretary of Defense for Intelligence, which is responsible for overseeing DOD's personnel security program, stated that their oversight efforts have been hindered by the lack of available data in JPAS, and that they do not have access to the component-specific case-management systems. DMDC officials stated that JPAS and the different case-management systems are going to be replaced, by 2016

---

[30]76 Fed. Reg. 24863 (May 3, 2011). DMDC officials stated that a new draft system of record notice for JPAS has been developed, but has not yet been approved for publication.

[31]In an April 2009 memorandum, the Under Secretary of Defense for Intelligence designated the Army's case management system as the DOD non-intelligence community system for case management and adjudication, and identified it as the preferred solution for receiving investigations and performing initial adjudications. However, this memorandum only designates this system for performing initial adjudications, and does not specify where adjudication appeals information should be recorded. Moreover, this memorandum precedes the May 2011 JPAS system of record designation, which states that JPAS includes records documenting the personnel security adjudicative and management process. DOD CAF officials explained that the different versions of the case management systems will be replaced by a single case management system by the end of fiscal year 2014.

and the end of fiscal year 2014, respectively. ODNI officials stated that it would be important for DOD to improve the data in JPAS before the new systems are implemented.

DOD is already aware that data in JPAS are not being updated as frequently as needed. For example, the November 2013 DOD report in response to the Navy Yard shooting found that DOD does not have policies addressing roles, responsibilities, and standards for security managers to ensure the upkeep of data in JPAS.[32] The report recommended that the department establish, reinforce, and enforce roles and responsibilities for updates to JPAS. Similarly, in April 2014, the DOD Inspector General issued a report assessing the personnel security clearance processes for contractors in four defense intelligence agencies. This report found a lack of effective recordkeeping that occurred because the appropriate investigative and personnel security databases, including JPAS, were not being reliably populated with investigative and security information. The report recommended that the Under Secretary of Defense for Intelligence direct the defense intelligence agencies to review the procedures used to ensure that JPAS and other systems are being properly populated. The report also found that DOD did not have any overarching policy documents governing JPAS operation, and recommended that DOD develop and issue an overarching policy for JPAS.[33] DOD officials acknowledged that the department needed to improve the data in JPAS. Until DOD takes steps to ensure that information is recorded and updated in its systems, the department will continue to lack visibility over the security clearance revocation and appeal process, which may hinder its ability to effectively oversee these processes.

[32]DOD, *Internal Review of the Washington Navy Yard Shooting*, p. 41.

[33]Department of Defense, Inspector General, *An Assessment of Contractor Personnel Security Clearance Processes in the Four Defense Intelligence Agencies*, DODIG-2014-060 (Apr. 14, 2014), p. 4.

Inconsistent Implementation of Revocation Requirements across DHS and DOD Is Due in Part to Limited Oversight of the Security Clearance Revocation Process

Inconsistent implementation of the requirements in the governing executive orders by DHS, DOD, and some of their components, and limited oversight over the revocation process, have resulted in employees in some agency components and workforces experiencing different protections and processes than employees in other agency components and workforces. DHS and DOD have implemented the requirements in Executive Orders 12968 and 10865 in different ways for different groups of personnel, but these differences are required or permitted by the executive orders. However, some components' implementation of the clearance revocation process could potentially be inconsistent with the executive orders in two areas: having an opportunity to be provided with certain information upon which a revocation appeal determination is based, and communicating the right to counsel. Although DHS and DOD have performed some oversight over the revocation process at the component level, they have not evaluated the quality of the process or developed performance measures to measure quality department-wide. Finally, while ODNI has exercised oversight of security clearance revocations by reviewing policies and procedures within some agencies, ODNI has not established any metrics to measure the quality of the process government-wide and has not reviewed revocation processes across the federal government to determine the extent to which policies and procedures should be uniform.

DHS and DOD Have Implemented Executive Order Requirements in Different Ways

DHS and DOD have implemented some requirements in the governing executive orders in different ways for different groups of personnel, but these differences are required or permitted by the executive orders. The areas of inconsistency include implementation of the personal appearance requirement, cross-examination of witnesses, and administration of the appeal boards within DOD.

DHS and DOD Implementation of Personal Appearance Requirement Provides Different Protection for Contractors than Military and Civilian Personnel

The right to a personal appearance during the personnel security clearance revocation process has been implemented differently across the two departments in a manner that provides different protections for contractors than for military and civilian personnel in two areas: the timing of the personal appearance and the information provided to the employee about the rationale supporting the revocation decision and the effect of the personal appearance. Executive Order 12968 provides that employees shall be provided an opportunity to appear personally at some point in the process before an adjudicative or other authority; it does not specify when during the process this personal appearance should occur. Executive Order 10865 provides that a contractor shall be provided an opportunity to appear personally after he or she has provided a written reply to the proposal to revoke eligibility to access classified information. Defense Office of Hearings and Appeals officials explained that the personal appearance is a significant opportunity to refute, explain, extenuate or mitigate critical facts, and stated that the later timing of this significant procedural protection for military and civilian personnel can adversely affect the individual's continued employment while the appeal process is completed.

The timing of the personal appearance for contractors is earlier in the revocation process than for DHS employees and DOD military and civilian employees. Contractors who receive a proposal to revoke their clearance may choose to respond to the proposal by requesting a personal appearance before an administrative judge. The administrative judge, in turn, issues a written decision to revoke or sustain the clearance after the employee has had his or her hearing. The contractor can appeal this decision to an appeal board. Thus, contractors have their personal appearance before the revocation decision is made. In contrast, military and civilian personnel within DHS and DOD who receive a notice that their clearance may be revoked can only submit written documentation prior to a revocation decision. Adjudicators issue a written decision to revoke or sustain the clearance before any personal appearance by, and without any in-person discussion with, the employee. The employee can appeal this written decision and request a personal appearance during the appeal process.

Furthermore, DHS military and civilian employees, and contractor employees government-wide, have a better opportunity than DOD military and civilian employees to understand the rationale for the revocation decision and the effect their personal appearance may have had on the revocation decision. DHS military and civilian employees receive a written decision letter to revoke or sustain the clearance from the individual who presided over the personal appearance. Similarly, contractors government-wide are also provided a copy of the administrative judge's written decision. However, for DOD military and civilian employees, the administrative judge who presided over the personal appearance during the appeal makes a written recommendation rather than a decision. This recommendation is sent directly to one of DOD's Personnel Security Appeals Boards (PSAB), based on the agency to which the employee is assigned, and the recommendation generally is not shared with the DOD military or civilian employee. The DOD PSABs consider the administrative judge's recommendation and other evidence when they reach and issue a final written decision regarding the security clearance to the employee, but they are not required to follow the judge's recommendation. The employee is provided a final written decision from one of the three military department PSABs, which cannot be appealed, but the employee generally is not privy to the administrative judge's recommendation. An exception is the Washington Headquarters Services appeal board which, in its written decision, typically provides the employee with a copy of the administrative judge's recommendation and the hearing transcript. Army PSAB officials explained that providing the judge's recommendation to the employee could be misleading because the individual might assume that was the final decision, and would be disappointed if the PSAB reached a different decision.

The level of detail contained in the written decisions received by employees after the personal appearance also varied, with contractors having more information about the rationale for the decision than military and federal civilian personnel in the military departments. When we reviewed Defense Office of Hearings and Appeals administrative judge decisions that are provided to contractors, we found that they contained detailed findings of fact, discussions of applicable law and policy, and analysis, which provides an employee an in-depth understanding of the rationale for the judge's decision. In reviewing versions of the PSAB decisions that are provided to military and civilian employees, however, we found that the Army and Air Force PSAB decisions were in a short memorandum format that state that case records have been reviewed and the board either sustains the revocation decision or reinstates eligibility for access to classified information. We found that only the Navy PSAB decisions provided a more detailed explanation of the rationale for the revocation of a security clearance. DOD guidance states that the PSAB's written decision will provide the reasons that the PSAB either sustained or overturned the original determination of the adjudication facility, and that the PSAB's final written determination shall state its rationale.[34]

According to Defense Office of Hearings and Appeals officials, DOD's process for its military and civilian workers provides less transparency, quality, and accountability compared to contractor personnel. Specifically, these officials stated that DOD's process for military and civilian employees makes it difficult to determine by reviewing the decision how

---

[34]DOD Regulation 5200.2-R, *Personnel Security Program*, Appendices 12 and 13, sections 12.1.8 and 13.1.6 respectively (January 1987, incorporating administrative change Feb. 23, 1996).

GAO-14-640 Security Clearance Revocations

or why component PSAB cases are decided the way they are. The officials also stated that they would like more transparency with regard to whether the component PSABs agreed or not with the administrative judge's recommendation, and stated that as of summer 2013, they are now able to track this information.

DHS and DOD Employees Experience Different Rights to Cross-examine Witnesses during the Revocation Process

DHS and DOD employees are provided different rights to present and cross-examine witnesses during personal appearances, as the departments have implemented the executive orders differently, resulting in contractors, DOD employees, and some DHS employees receiving greater opportunities to cross-examine witnesses than other DHS employees. Executive Order 10865 explicitly provides contractors the opportunity to cross-examine persons who have made oral or written statements adverse to the employee, subject to certain exceptions. In contrast, Executive Order 12968, which covers military and civilian employees and contractors, is silent on the opportunity to do so. DOD military and civilian employees are permitted to cross-examine witnesses according to a memorandum from the Under Secretary of Defense for Intelligence issued in November 2007.[35] Officials from the Defense Office of Hearings and Appeals and the Office of the Under Secretary of Defense for Intelligence stated that this was done as a matter of fundamental fairness, to give military and civilian employees an opportunity that had been provided to contractors for years.

However, the applicable DHS instruction is vague on this topic and has been interpreted by some DHS components to allow cross-examination of witnesses, while other DHS components do not permit cross-examination. The DHS instruction states that the personal appearance "proceeding need not allow for the testimony or cross-examination of witnesses."[36] This language has led to different witness testimony and cross-examination opportunities at different DHS components. For example, according to DHS officials, employees at some DHS components—such as DHS Headquarters, U.S. Customs and Border Protection, Transportation Security Administration, U.S. Coast Guard, and U.S. Secret Service—have not been allowed to call or cross-examine

---

[35]Under Secretary of Defense for Intelligence Memorandum, *Amendment to DOD Regulation 5200.2-R to Delete Bar on Witnesses* (Nov. 19, 2007).

[36]DHS Instruction Handbook 121-01-007, *The Department of Homeland Security Personnel Suitability and Security Program* (June 2009).

witnesses during the personal appearance, while employees at other DHS components, such as U.S. Citizenship and Immigration Services and U.S. Immigration and Customs Enforcement, have been allowed to cross-examine witnesses during the personal appearance. U.S. Immigration and Customs Enforcement officials stated that employees were allowed to call and question witnesses during the personal appearance on a case-by-case basis. DHS officials from the Office of the Chief Security Officer told us that all employees should be treated the same across DHS's components. They said that they would clarify the wording in the instruction, a draft of which has been under revision for more than a year; however, the officials had not decided whether they would revise the instruction to allow or prohibit the testimony or cross-examination of witnesses, and they could not tell us when the revised instruction would be finalized. Until the processes are consistent for all employees, and such processes are finalized in an instruction, employees within DHS may continue to have different rights concerning cross-examination of witnesses during the revocation process, depending on which component they work for.

DOD and the Military Departments Disagree on Legal Authority, Risks, and Benefits of Consolidating Multiple Appeals Boards

Each of DOD's three military departments—of the Army, the Navy, and the Air Force—has a PSAB that reviews cases and makes final eligibility determinations for access to classified information for that department's military and civilian employees.[37] A fourth appeals board is administered by DOD's Washington Headquarters Services, which reviews civilian employee cases for all other DOD agencies. A fifth appeals board is administered by the Defense Office of Hearings and Appeals, which reviews cases for all contractors in the industrial security program, including DOD and DHS. We have previously reported that overlap occurs when programs have similar goals, devise similar strategies and activities to achieve those goals, or target similar users, and duplication occurs when two or more agencies or programs are engaged in the same activities or provide the same services to the same beneficiaries.[38] While

---

[37]DOD guidance provides for the establishment of eight PSABs: Army, Navy, Air Force, Joint Chiefs of Staff, National Security Agency, Defense Intelligence Agency, Washington Headquarters Services, and Defense Office of Hearings and Appeals. DOD Regulation 5200.2-R. The scope of our review excluded the intelligence community (National Security Agency and Defense Intelligence Agency) and the Joint Chiefs of Staff.

[38]GAO, *2012 Annual Report: Opportunities to Reduce Duplication, Overlap and Fragmentation, Achieve Savings, and Enhance Revenue,* GAO-12-342SP (Washington, D.C.: Feb, 28, 2012).

overlap in efforts may be appropriate in some instances, especially if agencies can leverage each others' efforts, in other instances overlap may be unintended, may be unnecessary, or may represent an inefficient use of U.S. government resources. DOD's multiple different PSABs could constitute inefficient overlap because more than one component within DOD provides the same service.

In 2010, the Secretary of Defense directed a series of initiatives designed to reduce duplication, overhead, and excess and instill a culture of savings and cost accountability across the department. As part of this initiative, in March 2011, the Secretary approved a recommendation to colocate and consolidate the overlapping security clearance appeal boards[39] with the Defense Legal Services Agency,[40] similar to the colocation and consolidation of the service adjudication activities that were previously directed by the base realignment and closure process and the Deputy Secretary of Defense. The Secretary directed a completion date of September 30, 2011, for this recommendation. However, this recommendation had not been implemented at the time of our review. A Defense Office of Hearings and Appeals official explained that this direction had not been cancelled, but it had not been implemented because of opposition from the military departments. Officials from the Navy PSAB stated that the direction had not been implemented because the PSABs had not received any instructions or guidance to implement this direction from the Defense Legal Services Agency. Similarly, the Army PSAB attributed the lack of action to a focus on completing the consolidation of DOD's adjudication facilities as well as the absence of policy direction from the Under Secretary of Defense for Intelligence.

An official from the Office of the Under Secretary of Defense for Intelligence explained that there has been an impasse since 2011 over a legal question regarding whether the PSAB consolidation directed by the Secretary of Defense is consistent with Executive Order 12968. Specifically, Army and Air Force PSAB officials stated that PSAB

---

[39]Security clearance appeals boards are also referred to as Personnel Security Appeal Boards (PSAB).

[40]The Defense Legal Services Agency is one of the defense agencies, and is under the authority, direction, and control of the General Counsel of the Department of Defense, who serves as the agency's Director. The Defense Office of Hearings and Appeals is the largest component of the Defense Legal Services Agency.

consolidation is not consistent with Executive Order 12968, explaining that the review proceedings outlined in the executive order provide an employee with revoked access to classified information the opportunity for a final appeal in writing to an agency head–appointed high-level panel. Army and Air Force PSAB officials stated that "agency head" refers to the Secretary of the Military Departments, not the Secretary of Defense. Air Force PSAB officials stated that the Secretary of Defense direction for PSAB consolidation would require modifying section 5.2 of Executive Order 12968, and that removing PSABs from the services would neither enhance due process nor national security. Air Force PSAB officials also explained that the procedures used to review the DOD efficiency proposals did not include the opportunity for the service Secretaries to review and comment, and thus the memo directing consolidation of the PSABs was signed before military department equities in maintaining their department PSABs were captured for consideration.

However, an official from the Defense Office of Hearings and Appeals explained that the term "agency head" as used in the executive order includes the Secretary of Defense. Further, an official from the Office of the Under Secretary of Defense for Intelligence explained that by law, the Secretary of Defense has authority, direction, and control over the Department of Defense,[41] to include the Secretaries of the military departments,[42] and the Secretary of Defense's efficiency decisions are decisions as the head of DOD and apply to all subordinate components of the department, including the Secretaries of the military departments. This official stated that the interpretation of the language in the executive order was ultimately a legal question. DOD guidance provides that the DOD General Counsel shall provide advice and guidance as to the legal sufficiency of procedures and standards involved in implementing the DOD personnel security program.[43]

In addition to the disagreement about the legal authority to consolidate the PSABs, there is disagreement within the department about the risks and benefits of implementing the Secretary of Defense direction to consolidate the PSABs. Officials from the Army, the Navy, and the Air

---

[41]10 U.S.C. § 113.

[42]See 10 U.S.C. §§ 3013(b), 5013(b), and 8013(b).

[43]DOD Instruction 5200.02, *DOD Personnel Security Program* (Mar. 21, 2014).

Force PSABs explained that consolidating PSABs would limit the military department Secretary's ability to consider circumstances and risk in light of that specific service's special or sensitive programs, missions, or needs. Washington Headquarters Services officials stated that separate PSABs were more likely to be sensitive to their component's special programs, missions, and needs than a central DOD PSAB. Air Force PSAB officials stated that, from their past experience, the DOD Consolidated Adjudications Facility's (CAF) statement of reasons for revoking access to classified information is often narrowly focused and fails to weigh all issues appropriately, and that in personal hearings the Defense Office of Hearings Appeals administrative judges sometimes fail to challenge statements made by employees that immediately raise flags with PSAB members based on their background and experience. They stated that with the DOD CAF making initial DOD-wide risk assessments for the military departments, the final revocation appeals should be decided by the individual departments.

In contrast, officials from the Office of the Under Secretary of Defense for Intelligence and the Defense Office of Hearings and Appeals agree that DOD PSAB consolidation is in keeping with the principles of reciprocity where risk is managed DOD-wide, not on a component basis. They stated that with the DOD CAF, the components have already lost their ability to manage risk with respect to favorable adjudications because the CAF is making those decisions for the component when personnel security clearances are initially granted. Officials from the Defense Office of Hearings and Appeals stated that the requirement that agencies grant clearance reciprocity[44] has removed the role that service-specific programs may play in clearance determinations that were completed by another agency. Officials from the Office of the Under Secretary of Defense for Intelligence explained that consolidation would bring standardization and consistency of quality, objectivity, and experience to the process for personnel security appeals, and would result in legal expertise being part of every appeal process, which would help ensure that national security needs and procedural fairness are appropriately balanced. Further, Defense Office of Hearings and Appeals officials

---

[44]In this context, reciprocity means that executive-branch agencies must accept a background investigation or personnel security clearance determination completed by any authorized investigative or adjudicative agency, subject to certain exceptions. See The Intelligence Reform and Terrorism Prevention Act of 2004, Pub. L. No. 108-458, § 3001 (2004) (codified at 50 U.S.C. § 3341).

stated that contractors have the benefit of independent fact-finding and an independent written decision by officials who do not work for the component, which provides an important check against unfairness and the taint of undue influence. These officials stated that having decision makers outside of the component's chain of command helps to reduce the opportunity for the perception or reality that those in the individual's component or chain of command can influence the outcome of the process.

Officials from the DOD CAF cautioned that DOD needs to study the implications of moving to a consolidated appeal board to make an informed decision on any process modifications, efficiencies, and resource implications prior to executing the direction to consolidate the appeal boards. Army officials also suggested that establishment of a working group to review the efficiencies, feasibility, way ahead, and timelines would be beneficial in formulating a course of action in implementing the direction to consolidate the PSABs. Until DOD General Counsel resolves the disagreement within the department about the legal authority to consolidate the PSABs, and collaborates with the PSABs and the Under Secretary of Defense for Intelligence to address any other obstacles to consolidation, the department will continue to face delays implementing the Secretary of Defense's direction.

Implementation of Some Revocation Processes by Components Is Potentially Not Consistent with Executive Orders or Agency Policy

Our review of DHS and DOD department- and component-level guidance, as well as the components' communication letters to employees undergoing a revocation proceeding, found that both departments generally provided information to employees about their rights under the two executive orders. However, some components' implementation of the clearance revocation process could potentially be inconsistent with the executive orders or agency policy in two areas: having an opportunity to be provided any additional information upon which a revocation appeal determination is based, and communicating the right to counsel.

Navy and Army Policies Could Result in PSABs Collecting New Information without Sharing It with the Employee or Providing the Employee with an Opportunity to Respond

Navy and Army policies could allow the Navy and Army PSABs to collect and consider new information related to the revocation decision without informing the employee or giving the employee the opportunity to review or respond to the new information. For example, Navy Manual M-5510.30 strongly encourages the employee's command to submit additional information directly to the Navy PSAB after military and civilian personnel have made their personal appearance in front of the administrative judge.[45] This creates the potential for important information, upon which an appeal of a revocation decision might be denied, to be introduced without the individual's awareness. Executive Order 12968, however, states that employees who are determined not to meet the standards for access to classified information shall be provided with a reasonable opportunity to reply in writing to and request a review of the determination, and to request any documents, records, and reports upon which a revocation is based, to the extent that the documents would be provided under the Freedom of Information Act or Privacy Act.

Under the DOD regulation[46] and the Navy manual, this opportunity is provided to military and civilian personnel before the case reaches the PSAB. Accordingly, DOD officials explained that the Navy manual encourages submission of new information at a point in the process after the employee has received and responded to all information upon which the revocation was based. As a result, the Navy manual may be inconsistent with this provision of the executive order. The Navy manual is silent on whether the individual will be provided an opportunity to see the command's submission or address the information contained in it. A Navy PSAB official explained that, to ensure due process, both parties are informed, with the employee being informed through his or her agency security manager or point of contact. The official further stated that most commands do not provide a recommendation or position paper to the PSAB, but acknowledged that the Navy manual needs to be updated. Until the Navy manual is updated to specify that all information provided to the Navy PSAB by the command must also be shared with the individual, along with an opportunity to respond to this information, the Navy PSAB could potentially deny an employee some of the protections provided in the executive order.

---

[45]Secretary of the Navy Manual M-5510.30, *Department of the Navy Personnel Security Program* (June 2006), Chapter 8, § 8-5.3.i and 8-5.4.d (pages 8-11, 8-12), For cases where the individual elects a personal appearance, the guidance states that "commands are strongly encouraged to submit a position paper directly to the (Navy) Personnel Security Appeal Board." For cases where the individual elects to appeal directly in writing to the PSAB, the guidance states that "Commands will provide a command perspective by submitting an endorsement to the individual's written appeal."

[46]DOD Regulation 5200.2-R, *Personnel Security Program* (January 1987, incorporating administrative change Feb. 23, 1996).

GAO-14-640 Security Clearance Revocations

Similarly, Army Regulation 380-67 could allow the Army PSAB to collect information without informing the employee or giving the employee the opportunity to respond to the new information. The Army regulation regarding appeal of a revocation decision requires the employee to respond to the decision through his or her immediate commanding officer.[47] The Army regulation further requires that the commanding officer must recommend for or against reinstatement of the security clearance, and provide a rationale addressing the issues in the decision. As written, the Army regulation is silent on whether the comments will be provided to the individual to review and respond to the information contained in it. Army PSAB officials said that the PSAB is not responsible for providing employees with this information.

Further, Army PSAB officials noted that in cases where a security clearance was revoked because of financial considerations, the Army PSAB would request additional documentation concerning any actions that the employee has taken to resolve delinquent debts, but stated that the Army PSAB will obtain credit reports directly from the credit reporting bureaus and compare them to the documents in the appeal package. Army PSAB officials explained that the credit report is accessed solely to verify the existence or resolution of disqualifying financial information that formed the basis of an unfavorable determination by the DOD CAF, so it is not routinely provided to the employees, but they said that it would be provided upon request. This raises concerns about whether the employee has an opportunity to review or respond to information in the credit reports obtained directly by the PSAB, because credit reports may not always be accurate. Until the Army regulation is revised to specify that all information provided to the Army PSAB by the command or obtained by the Army PSAB itself must also be shared with the individual, along with an opportunity to respond to this information, the Army PSAB could potentially deny employees some of the protections provided in the executive order.

U.S. Coast Guard Did Not Communicate Right to Counsel to Its Military Personnel

DOD security clearance revocation prehearing memorandums provided to employees inform all types of employees—military personnel, DOD civilians, and contractors—of their right to obtain legal representation, and allow for discussion of any relevant issues. In contrast, at the time of our

---

[47]Army Regulation 380-67, *Personnel Security Program*, Chapter 8, § 8-6(b)(4) (August 2011).

review, one DHS component—the Coast Guard—was not notifying its military personnel of their right to be represented by counsel or other representative at their own expense, but rather was erroneously informing military personnel that they had no right to counsel. While Executive Order 12968 and DHS Instruction Handbook 121-01-007 specify that employees shall be informed of their right to be represented by counsel or other representative at their own expense, letters the Coast Guard sent its military personnel appealing to the second-level deciding authority stated "you may not have an attorney or anyone else with you during this administrative process." The existing Coast Guard Instruction states that if the final decision results in a revocation, the employee will be advised of his or her rights, but does not specify what these rights are.[48]

During our review, the Coast Guard Security Center Director acknowledged this disparity and stated the letters would be changed to provide the required notification to military personnel that they have a right to be represented by counsel or other representative at their own expense during the personal appearance before the second-level deciding authority. We subsequently reviewed a revised letter, and it had been modified to inform military personnel of their right to be represented by counsel. In addition, the Director said he would advocate for modifying the Coast Guard instruction to formalize this change. Currently, this Coast Guard instruction is undergoing revision, and the updated version is expected to be published in the fall of 2014. According to a Coast Guard official, the revised instruction will address this issue, but we have not reviewed the revision to determine whether this change was included.

In addition, although the Coast Guard's communication letters inform Coast Guard civilian employees of their right to be represented by counsel or other representative at their own expense during the personal appearance, they impose some stipulations. The Coast Guard letters, unlike those sent by other DHS components, state that only the employee's account of the issues can be heard during the meeting, the employee's counsel or representative cannot instruct the employee during the meeting, and the employee is limited to only 30 minutes to appear in person and present any relevant information. The Coast Guard Security Center Director said these stipulations are imposed because the intent is

---

[48]Department of Homeland Security, U.S. Coast Guard Commandant's Instruction M5520.12C, *Personnel Security and Suitability Program*, Chapter 3, § P.1 (Change 1 Mar. 18, 2010).

to avoid allowing the administrative review from becoming a protracted and adversarial legal proceeding where objections are injected or cross-examinations are sought. To his knowledge, the "30 minutes" has never been enforced and is now under review for removal from the Coast Guard instruction. However, until the Coast Guard instruction and related communication letters are revised to clearly and consistently communicate rights provided by the executive orders, military and civilian employees within the Coast Guard are at risk of not being treated similarly to one another or to employees in other DHS components.

DHS and DOD Have Performed Some Oversight over Revocation Process at Component Level but Have Not Evaluated Quality of Revocation Process at Department Level

DHS has taken recent steps in response to recommendations made in a December 2013 DHS Office of Inspector General report,[49] and individual DHS and DOD components perform some oversight over aspects of the revocation process. But neither department has performed an overarching, department-wide evaluation of the quality of the revocation process or has developed performance measures and collects data to measure the quality of the process.

DHS has taken some recent steps to improve the quality of the revocation process. Specifically, the DHS Office of Inspector General report found that appointments to the DHS Security Appeals Board and the composition of the board had not been made in accordance with DHS policy. For example, it found that one member[50] served on the Security Appeals Board when an employee in his chain of command was the appellant, even though DHS guidance provides that board members cannot have a current supervisory relationship with the employee whose appeal is being heard.[51] The Inspector General report recommended that

---

[49]Department of Homeland Security, Office of Inspector General, *Adequacy of USSS Efforts to Identify, Mitigate, and Address Instances of Misconduct and Inappropriate Behavior* (Redacted), OIG-14-20 (December 2013).

[50]The Assistant Chief of the Secret Service Uniformed Division is responsible for ensuring fairness in the administration of procedures with regard to discipline, and sees every discipline case and engages in discussions with his subordinates about what discipline should be proposed.

[51]DHS Instruction Handbook 121-01-007, *The Department of Homeland Security Personnel Suitability and Security Program* (June 18, 2009). All members of the board over the last 10 years have been Secret Service employees and thus were involved with the appeals cases of Secret Service employees. Nearly 30 percent (15 of 50) of the DHS cases that went to the appeals board from fiscal years 2011 through 2013 involved Secret Service employees, which could result in employees facing a board that might not be independent.

the Director of the U.S. Secret Service ensure that the Uniformed Division Assistant Chief, or other officials in the agency's chain of command, do not rule on appeals by Uniformed Division employees. In March 2014, the Secret Service issued a new directive describing the composition of the board and how a board member would be replaced if a case involved an employee in his or her chain of command.[52]

Further, some DHS component officials told us that their component provides oversight during the revocation process. For example, officials from U.S. Citizenship and Immigration Services said that revocation data are reviewed throughout the process, at the initial stage of determining whether the action is warranted and by management at the initial stage and each subsequent stage, and by legal counsel prior to approval and signature of the revocation letter. Similarly, at DHS Headquarters, U.S. Immigration and Customs Enforcement, and the Federal Emergency Management Agency, officials stated that revocation determinations undergo multiple stages of review, including by the adjudicator's first-line supervisor, the Personnel Security Division Director, and an attorney. Other components, such as Transportation Security Administration and DHS Headquarters, perform reviews after the process has been completed to determine whether policies and procedures were consistently followed prior to reaching the final case determination. In addition, DHS Headquarters officials said that they review all DHS component case files before the cases are sent to the Security Appeals Board.

Within DOD, although the Under Secretary of Defense for Intelligence is responsible for developing, coordinating, and overseeing the implementation of DOD policy, programs, and guidance for personnel security, the extent of oversight over the clearance revocation process and the use of related metrics varies across the department. Officials explained that the Office of the Under Secretary of Defense for Intelligence conducts annual quality reviews of DOD security clearance adjudicative determinations, but explained that their oversight efforts have been hindered by the lack of available data in JPAS, as we previously

---

[52]The new directive provides that two of the Security Appeals Board members can be either DHS or Secret Service employees, and must be outside the personnel security field. U.S. Secret Service, *Suspension, Denial, or Revocation of Access to Classified Information*, HRT-2014-16 (Mar. 14, 2014). This directive revises section RPS-02(02) of the Secret Service's Human Resources and Training Manual.

discussed. They explained that they do not have access to the agency-specific case-management systems, and that they have sent out manual data requests in the past, but have experienced difficulties in receiving responses to these requests that all have a consistent interpretation of the data. Furthermore, officials from the four PSABs we met with stated they collect appeal data—such as number of cases reviewed, favorable decisions, unfavorable issues, and number of days to process an appeal—and that they generated and submitted internal reports with this information to their respective leadership, but these appeal board officials did not elaborate how the information provided to their superiors was used to perform oversight.

ODNI Has Exercised Some Oversight over Security Clearance Revocations, but Has Not Reviewed the Extent That Clearance Revocation Process Should Be Uniform across the Federal Government

ODNI has exercised some oversight of security clearance revocations by reviewing policies and procedures within some agencies; however, it has not established any metrics to measure the quality of the process government-wide and has not reviewed security clearance revocation processes across the federal government to determine the extent to which policies and procedures should be uniform. In addition to DHS and DOD, ODNI also has oversight responsibility for the security clearance process government-wide. In June 2008, Executive Order 13467[53] designated the DNI as the Security Executive Agent to, among other things, direct the oversight of determinations of eligibility for access to classified information or to hold a sensitive position, and assigned the DNI responsibility for developing uniform and consistent policies and procedures to ensure the effective, efficient, and timely completion of investigations and adjudications relating to determinations of eligibility for access to classified information or to hold a sensitive position. Executive Order 13467 also provides the DNI the authority to issue guidelines and instructions to the heads of agencies to ensure appropriate uniformity, centralization, efficiency, effectiveness, and timeliness in processes relating to determinations by agencies of eligibility for access to classified information or eligibility to hold a sensitive position. This executive order further states that agency heads shall assist in carrying out any function

[53]Executive Order 13467, *Reforming Processes Related to Suitability for Government Employment, Fitness for Contractor Employees, and Eligibility for Access to Classified National Security Information* (June 30, 2008).

GAO-14-640 Security Clearance Revocations

under the order, which includes implementing any policies or procedures developed pursuant to the order.[54]

ODNI has exercised some oversight of security clearance revocations to determine whether the processes are being followed. ODNI officials explained that they have reviewed personnel security clearance revocation policies and processes within select agencies to determine the extent that agencies are in compliance with current laws and executive orders. In particular, ODNI officials said that they have conducted seven joint reviews of the security clearance process, along with the Office of Personnel Management (OPM),[55] between April 2013 and June 2014. Although these reviews are not specifically focused on the revocation process, ODNI officials stated that these reviews look at the entire security clearance process, to include security clearance revocations. In April 2014, ODNI issued a memo that formally established this review process, called the Security Executive Agent National Assessments Program. In addition, ODNI is developing a survey for agencies as part of this program to help ODNI ensure that agencies' policies are consistent with national security and there is fairness in the processes. ODNI officials said the survey is currently in testing and that it is expected to be launched across the federal government at the end of fiscal year 2014. A draft of this survey contained one question about clearance revocations, asking agencies to enumerate how many revocations resulted from continuous evaluation activities. ODNI officials said that a subsequent draft of the survey included a separate section, with six questions, that

---

[54]Executive Order 12968 assigns agency heads responsibility to direct and administer the agency's personnel security program and to promulgate policies and processes for access determinations and revocations consistent with national policy. Executive Order No. 12968, *Access to Classified Information* (Aug. 2, 1995, as amended). ODNI officials explained that this means that agency heads may disagree with ODNI prescribing specific processes that do not align to the structure of their agency, processes, or mission. They also stated that while ODNI does not mandate that agencies follow specific processes, ODNI is tasked with ensuring that each agency promulgates policies that are not only fair, but are consistent with national security.

[55]Executive Order 13467 designated the Director of OPM as the Suitability Executive Agent, responsible for developing and implementing uniform and consistent policies and procedures to ensure the effective, efficient, and timely completion of investigations and adjudications relating to determinations of suitability for government employment. Executive Order 13467, *Reforming Processes Related to Suitability for Government Employment, Fitness for Contractor Employees, and Eligibility for Access to Classified National Security Information* (June 30, 2008).

was added to address an agency's process to deny or revoke a clearance.

Despite these efforts at the component level, neither DHS, DOD, nor ODNI have evaluated the quality of the revocation process across the specific departments or government-wide. DHS and DOD do not perform overarching, department-wide oversight over the revocation process, and neither department has developed metrics or collected data to measure the quality of the revocation process. Furthermore, ODNI officials acknowledged that metrics have not been established to measure the quality of the security clearance revocation process. In November 2013, we testified that executive-branch agencies do not consistently assess quality throughout the personnel security clearance process, in part because they have not fully developed and implemented metrics to measure quality in key aspects of the personnel security clearance process.[56] Having assessment tools and performance metrics in place is a critical initial step toward instituting a program to monitor and independently validate the effectiveness and sustainability of corrective measures. Our work has also found that agency managers need performance information as a basis for decision making to improve programs and results, identify problems in existing programs and develop corrective actions, and identify priorities and make resource decisions.[57]

ODNI officials stated that they currently report some limited metrics on revocations for the intelligence community as part of their reporting in response to the Intelligence Authorization Act for Fiscal Year 2010.[58] They said that they would like to establish and make more robust metrics for reciprocity, quality, and out-of-scope periodic reinvestigations, and from there it would be a natural progression to look at developing some metrics for revocations and denials, and other areas. However, they stated that due to constrained resources and other priorities they were uncertain whether they could make a business case to allocate the resources. The absence of data on the number of persons who receive a

---

[56]GAO, *Personnel Security Clearances: Opportunities Exist to Improve Quality Throughout the Process*, GAO-14-186T (Nov. 13, 2013).

[57]GAO, *Managing for Results: Enhancing Agency Use of Performance Information for Management Decision Making*, GAO-05-927 (Sept. 9, 2005).

[58]The Intelligence Authorization Act for Fiscal Year 2010, Pub. L. No. 111-259, § 367 (2010) (codified in relevant part at 50 U.S.C. § 3104).

proposal to revoke their eligibility to access classified information, as discussed above, combined with the likelihood that the shift to increase continuous evaluation may result in increased instances of revocation proposals, make it increasingly important for agencies to have performance measures and data to ensure a high-quality revocation process. Without performance measures and data to assess the quality of the personnel security clearance revocation process, individual departments, such as DHS and DOD, and ODNI lack information to identify and resolve potential problems in the process, and make informed decisions about potential changes to the program.

Furthermore, the security clearance revocation process implementation differences we identified at DHS and DOD continue in part because ODNI has not reviewed security clearance revocation processes across the federal government to determine the extent to which policies and procedures should be uniform. Specifically, ODNI has not assessed whether the existing security clearance framework, with its parallel processes for contractors and government employees, or a single process applicable to all types of employees would best facilitate the effective, efficient, consistent, and timely completion of security clearance revocation proceedings. When asked about the different processes, ODNI officials stated that the executive orders provide broad guidelines that give agencies the flexibility to implement a review and appeal process that best fits the agency's needs, and there is no single solution that all agencies must follow. Additionally, Executive Orders 12968 and 10865 do not require a uniform government-wide process, and in fact establish two parallel processes, one for contractors and one for government employees.[59] The ODNI officials explained that from an efficiencies perspective, standardization of the security clearance revocation process makes sense, but said that ODNI has not had a reason or purpose to perform an extensive review of the revocation processes. The ODNI officials stated that they had not heard complaints regarding fairness while conducting their reviews, and had only heard anecdotal concerns that the process took too long. Furthermore, ODNI has not established any policies and procedures to facilitate government-wide consistency in security clearance revocation proceedings. ODNI officials stated that

---

[59]The requirements of executive orders 10865 and 12968, which govern the personnel security clearance revocation processes, were established in 1960 and 1995, respectively, prior to DNI's designation as the security executive agent responsible for oversight of the process. Since that designation, the DNI's role has evolved as it began executing its new responsibilities.

publishing guidance for the appeal process might be worth pursuing, but would have to be prioritized in light of competing priorities and limited resources. Given the inconsistencies we have identified in the revocation processes at DHS and DOD discussed previously, combined with the requirement of clearance reciprocity and the recommendations to implement continuous evaluation, the DNI's new role as Security Executive Agent places ODNI in a unique position to examine whether any changes to the existing structure with its parallel revocation processes might be warranted. Until ODNI reviews the effectiveness and efficiency of all aspects of the security clearance revocation process, and DHS and DOD take specific actions, it is difficult to determine whether the existing structures, with different processes for military and civilian personnel and for contractors, are the most appropriate approach to meet national security needs.

Employment Outcomes after Clearance Revocation Are Determined Based on Several Factors, and Identification of these Outcomes Is Hindered by Lack of Data

DHS and DOD employees whose eligibility to access classified information has been revoked may not have consistent employment outcomes, such as reassignment or termination, because these outcomes are generally dependent on several factors, including the agency's mission and needs and the manager's discretion. Communication between personnel security and human capital offices at DHS and DOD varies, because human capital and personnel security processes are intentionally managed separately, and most components could not readily ascertain the employment outcomes of individuals whose clearances had been revoked.

Employment Outcomes for DHS and DOD Employees with Revoked Clearances Generally Is at Discretion of Employee's Supervisor or Commander

Employment outcomes, such as reassignment or termination, for DHS and DOD civilian and military employees whose personnel security clearance has been revoked are generally dependent on a number of factors, including the agency's mission and needs. Key to the decision is the judgment of the employee's supervisor or commander, and also whether there is a job available that the employee is qualified to perform and the supervisor or commander considers it appropriate or possible to reassign the employee. DHS officials elaborated that if an individual's clearance was revoked, then he or she is no longer qualified to perform the job he or she was hired for, and so, depending on the policies at the component where the employee works, the agency may have no obligation to reassign the individual to another position or find another position for the employee. DOD officials stated that in many places within the department, all positions are sensitive, so there may be no positions to which an employee could be reassigned. DHS officials stated that in such agencies where all positions require a clearance, holding a clearance is usually a condition of employment.

Components within DHS and DOD varied as to whether they reassign an employee after a security clearance revocation. Officials from five DHS components—U.S. Customs and Border Protection, U.S. Citizenship and Immigration Services, U.S. Coast Guard, U.S. Immigration and Customs Enforcement, and Transportation Security Administration—stated that management at their component could decide whether to reassign a civilian employee to a position with duties not requiring access to classified information. For two DHS components, U.S. Secret Service and DHS Headquarters, reassignment is generally not an option because all or almost all positions in these components require a security clearance. A DHS Headquarters general counsel official stated that DHS has no official policy regarding reassignment, so that it can preserve its administrative options. However, for DHS military personnel, Coast Guard officials said their component has guidance stating that in cases where a clearance is terminated for cause and the employee is not recommended for separation from the Coast Guard, the employee will be reassigned to a position that does not require a security clearance.

For most DOD civilian and military personnel, officials said that supervisors or commanders have discretionary authority to determine how to treat employees whose security clearance has been revoked. For DOD civilian employees, Army, Air Force, Marine Corps, and Washington Headquarters Services officials stated that supervisors have discretion to reassign employees, while Navy officials said that civilian employees will undergo a removal action after all appeals are completed if access to classified information is revoked. Additionally, while DOD department-level and Air Force guidance does not require separation of officers whose clearances have been revoked, with DOD guidance stating that officers may be separated from military service,[60] Army and Navy

---

[60]DOD Instruction 1332.30, *Separation of Regular and Reserve Commissioned Officers*, Enclosure 2, § 3 (Nov. 25, 2013); Air Force Instruction 36-2101, *Classifying Military Personnel (Officer and Enlisted)*, section 4.1 (June 25, 2013, incorporating change 1 Nov. 18, 2013).

guidance requires the discharge of an officer who receives a final revocation of a security clearance.[61] However, two Army regulations concerning officers appear to contradict each other. While one Army regulation states that revocation of an officer's security clearance requires that the officer be discharged, and further states that this requirement cannot be waived,[62] a different Army regulation regarding reassignment of officers provides guidance for the reassignment of officers whose security clearance has been revoked.[63]

For enlisted military personnel whose security clearance has been revoked, officials from the military services stated that the Army and the Marine Corps reassign military personnel to the extent that an alternative position is available, and the Air Force may reassign military personnel, while the Navy will generally only reassign military personnel until a final revocation decision is made by the PSAB.[64] Army officials noted, however, that a clearance revocation should affect a soldier's ability to reenlist, because as of 2005 all soldiers enlisting in the Army are subject to an investigation for eligibility to access classified information at the secret level, regardless of the access requirements of their position. Navy officials said that since 2011, all Navy positions require secret clearance eligibility as a condition of employment, regardless of whether the position

---

[61]Army Regulation 600-8-24, *Personnel-General: Officer Transfers and Discharges*, Chapter 4 § 4-1(c) (Apr. 12, 2006, Rapid Action Revision Sept. 13, 2011); Navy Personnel Command (NAVPERS) 15560D, *Naval Military Personnel Manual*, Article 1301-227, § 1.b. (Aug. 22, 2002, incorporating changes through Apr. 24, 2013).

[62]Army Regulation 600-8-24, *Personnel-General: Officer Transfers and Discharges*, Chapter 4, § 4-1(c) (Apr. 12, 2006, Rapid Action Revision Sept. 13, 2011).

[63]Army Regulation 614-100, *Officer Assignment Policies, Details, and Transfers*, Chapter 5, § 5-1(b)(5) (Jan. 10, 2006).

[64]Washington Headquarters Services officials explained that they do not make employment decisions regarding military personnel. Upon notification of a security clearance revocation, the agency would return the servicemember to his or her respective service, which would then determine the appropriate action.

GAO-14-640 Security Clearance Revocations

requires access to classified information. As a result, a sailor who has lost his or her security clearance generally will be separated from the Navy.[65]

Given the component's policies and procedures regarding reassignment, officials from four DHS components—U.S. Citizenship and Immigration Services, U.S. Customs and Border Protection, U.S. Immigration and Customs Enforcement, and Transportation Security Administration—told us that it would be possible for similarly situated employees under investigation for the same infraction to be treated differently if their clearances were revoked. When asked how the quality of the process could be improved once a final revocation decision has been made, Immigration and Customs Enforcement officials suggested that the agency could identify a single human capital deciding official to review all employment outcomes, to ensure consistency of employment status decisions across the agency. The officials explained that knowing and tracking the employment outcomes of individuals who lost their clearances would benefit the agency, because disparate treatment would not be an appropriate outcome. For DHS Headquarters and the Secret Service, which do not reassign personnel whose clearances have been revoked, all employees will be treated similarly because employees who lose their clearances will be terminated. Given the varying policies and procedures at DOD components, similarly situated civilian and military personnel whose security clearances have been revoked may be treated differently.

Communication Varies between Personnel Security and Human Capital Offices

Communication between personnel security and human capital offices at DHS and DOD varies, but lack of communication between these offices could result in adverse employment actions being taken prematurely or in inappropriate use of personnel security or human capital processes. According to DHS and DOD officials, the personnel security revocation processes and human capital disciplinary or adverse action processes are intended to be separate and distinct processes, to help ensure independence and protect national security. DHS and DOD officials stated that an adverse disciplinary personnel action could be taken based on the same underlying offense that led to the revocation proceeding, and

---

[65]Navy officials also explained that this change has had a detrimental effect on the Navy's ability to retain foreign nationals who are servicemembers. They explained that there are a large number of foreign national servicemembers in the Navy; however, foreign nationals do not have clearance eligibility. As a result, the requirement that all positions require secret clearance eligibility has created complications for the Navy in handling these servicemembers.

if that were to occur, the misconduct and personnel security processes can run in parallel or they can run consecutively. However, after a final decision is made to revoke a personnel security clearance, DHS and DOD personnel security officials said that their role in the process is over, and that it is a human capital decision as to what next happens to the individual. A DHS Headquarters general counsel official further stated that any personnel actions that result due to the revocation of a personnel security clearance are based exclusively on the fact that the individual is no longer qualified for his or her position, not on the reasons underlying the revocation action.

Good human capital policies and practices, to include appropriate practices for evaluating, counseling, and disciplining personnel, are critical factors that affect the quality of internal controls. Moreover, to run and control operations and achieve goals, agencies must have relevant, reliable, and timely communications relating to internal as well as external events; effective communications should occur in a broad sense, with information flowing down, across, and up the organization.[66] Personnel security offices at some DHS and DOD components said they worked very closely with human capital officials throughout the personnel security clearance revocation process, while at other components there was very little interaction between the offices. For example, Secret Service officials said that they have excellent communication between the personnel security and the human capital offices, and that personnel from both offices meet at every step of the process. Similarly, Coast Guard officials stated that their human capital and personnel security offices work closely with each other throughout the revocation process with respect to civilian employees.

In contrast, Immigration and Customs Enforcement officials stated that they are unaware of any specific DHS human capital policies and procedures that align or support the security process. These officials also stated that better coordination and communication between human capital and personnel security offices is needed during the revocation process, and that increased coordination and communication could improve the quality of the process. Similarly, DHS Headquarters employee relations officials said that their office is not involved or

---

[66]GAO, *Standards for Internal Control in the Federal Government*, GAO-AIMD-00-21.3.1 (November 1999), pp. 9-10, pp. 18-19.

informed by the personnel security office throughout the security revocation and appeal process, which includes the initial decision to revoke an employee's security clearance through the three levels of appeal. They explained that their office gets involved after the decision to revoke the employee's security clearance is final, and the human capital office communicates with the personnel security office when a personnel action is necessary. They explained that this communication is not to share the details of the underlying offense, but to notify the human capital office or supervisor of the status of the investigation. An official from the DHS Office of General Counsel stated that the office is involved throughout the revocation process to provide legal sufficiency reviews of clearance determinations and to advise management during any clearance-related personnel action.

Within DOD, Army human capital officials stated that the appropriate offices are not informed of the revocation of the security clearance due to weaknesses in information sharing with other Army offices. They explained that there is no standard time frame or process for the civilian personnel office to be notified about a civilian employee's clearance revocation, but the office is typically notified when the supervisor seeks advice regarding what action to take now that the employee's clearance has been revoked. In contrast, Navy human capital officials stated that the nature of the adverse information may trigger employee misconduct actions as well as actions to revoke a security clearance, thus making communication among the commanding officer, security manager, and the serving human resource office essential. They said that, generally, the security officer and the human resource office interact at all stages of the incident. Similarly, Marine Corps headquarters officials stated that its human resources office works with the local command and includes its local security manager into the process from the very beginning of the revocation process. Air Force officials stated the local human capital office is normally informed by the organization when the employee's security clearance is revoked. Washington Headquarters Services human capital officials stated that their personnel security office and occasionally the local component security manager notifies their human capital office when an employee's security clearance has been revoked.

A lack of communication between the human capital and personnel security offices could result in adverse employment actions being taken prematurely or in the inappropriate use of personnel security processes in lieu of human capital processes. For example, DOD officials stated that one issue that can arise is that human capital officials could fire an individual before all of the appeals associated with a revocation action are completed. If the termination was based upon a separate adverse action proceeding, that action would be appropriate; however, if the action was based on the clearance revocation, then, under DOD regulation, subject to certain exceptions, termination should not take place until after the revocation decision is final, after all appeals have been completed.[67] Defense Office of Hearings and Appeals and other DOD officials stated that some components are inappropriately terminating employees due to loss of a security clearance before the personnel security clearance appeal process is completed. In addition, ODNI officials explained that some agencies could use the personnel security process to handle personnel disciplinary issues, which is not appropriate. For example, Defense Office of Hearings and Appeals Officials said that retaliation against whistleblowers is perceived, fairly or not, as a continuing problem in the personnel security clearance arena. Ordinarily, most federal civilian employees[68] have a right to appeal serious adverse employment actions[69] taken against them to the Merit Systems Protections Board. However, in the security clearance context, federal case law[70] has limited the scope of the board's review of adverse actions. Specifically, the board may review appeals of adverse employment actions resulting from a denial or revocation of a security clearance or a determination that an employee is not eligible to hold a sensitive position for specific procedural issues,[71] but the board cannot review the substance of a security clearance denial or revocation, or a finding that an employee is not eligible to hold a sensitive position. DOD officials said that the personnel security and human capital processes are designed and intended to be

---

[67]DOD Regulation 5200.2-R, *Personnel Security Program* (January 1987, incorporating administrative change Feb. 23, 1996).

[68]The specific categories of federal civilian employees eligible to appeal adverse actions to the Merit Systems Protection Board vary to some extent depending on the status of the employee and the action being appealed.

[69]The adverse actions that may be appealed include, among other things: removals, suspensions of more than 14 days, reductions in grade or pay, furloughs of 30 days or less, performance-based removals or reductions in grade, denials of within-grade salary increases, reduction-in-force actions, and OPM suitability determinations.

[70]See *Department of Navy v. Egan*, 484 U.S. 518 (1988), and *Kaplan v. Conyers*, 733 F.3d 1148 (Fed. Cir. 2013), cert. denied by *Northover v. Archuleta*, 134 S.Ct. 1759 (Mar. 31, 2014).

[71]For example, the Merit Systems Protection Board may review, among other things, whether the clearance was actually denied or revoked, whether the employee received certain procedural protections, or whether a transfer to a nonsensitive position was feasible.

separate in part to protect the employee from someone trying to exercise undue influence over the disciplinary process, as well as to protect national security. ODNI officials stated that there are legal restrictions on the type of information that can be shared between the human capital and personnel security offices, but said that further review of what information should be shared between the two offices could be beneficial. Until DHS and DOD develop guidance specifying what information can and should be communicated between human capital and personnel security officials, and at what decision points during the revocation process that information should be communicated, DHS and DOD will be hampered in their ability to combat the perception that the personnel security process is being used to circumvent procedural protections ordinarily provided to federal employees subject to adverse employment actions, and that individuals are not being treated in a fair and consistent manner.

DHS and DOD Do Not Readily Know Employment Outcomes of Individuals with Revoked Clearances Because Data Are Not Readily Available

DOD and most DHS components cannot readily ascertain the employment outcomes of individuals whose clearances had been revoked, because these data are not readily available. Within DOD, officials representing all DOD civilian and military personnel—in the Army, the Navy, the Marine Corps, the Air Force, and Washington Headquarters Services[72]—stated that they do not track and would not be able to report the human capital outcomes of employees with revoked security clearances. For example, Army officials explained that there is a resignation code in their human capital database, but that code covers all resignations for any reason, and there may or may not be a remark on the agency's personnel action form (known as an SF-50) that would relate the resignation to a security clearance issue. Moreover, Army officials explained that if an individual were removed as a result of a security clearance revocation, the removal code could be attributed to failing to meet any one of several conditions of employment, if maintaining eligibility for a security clearance was one of the requirements listed in an individual's position description. An official from the Office of the Under Secretary of Defense for Personnel and Readiness explained that the separation codes applied for military personnel are similarly broad in nature, and would include separations for reasons other than revocation of a security clearance.

---

[72]Washington Headquarters Services officials explained that they do not make employment decisions regarding military personnel. Upon notification of a security clearance revocation, the agency would return the servicemember to their respective service, who would then determine the appropriate action.

Officials in some DHS components said they could manually gather information about employment outcomes from clearance revocations, but they explained that doing this would be labor-intensive because their human capital system would need to be cross-referenced against the personnel security system. For example, U.S. Immigration and Customs Enforcement officials commented that there is no DHS or Immigration and Customs Enforcement policy that requires the collection of data and reporting of outcomes for employees with revoked security clearances, but stated that they could determine the employment outcomes on a piecemeal basis by making a data query for each employee record. However, Coast Guard officials said that they maintain a spreadsheet of all disciplinary and adverse actions taken against its civilian employees. Similarly, Transportation Security Administration personal security officials also stated that their component can identify the outcomes of employees with revoked security clearances with help from human capital officials.

Data ODNI Provides to Congress on Total Employees Eligible for Access to Classified Information May Include Inaccurate DOD Data

The Intelligence Authorization Act for Fiscal Year 2010 requires the President to submit an annual report to Congress on, among other things, the total number of personnel security clearances across the government, categorized by government employees and contractors who held or were approved for a security clearance.[73] In response to this requirement, ODNI has prepared and submitted a report each year, with the most recent report being issued for fiscal year 2013. However, we found that the DOD data that are included in this report to Congress likely overstate the total number of DOD employees eligible to access classified information, in part because JPAS does not have up-to-date information about the current population of DOD employees. Without accurate data, DOD's ability to reduce the total population of clearance holders and minimize risk and reduce costs to the government will be hampered. To measure performance, it is important that organizations have sufficiently complete, accurate, and consistent data to document performance and support decision making. Further, one of the five internal control standards that define the minimum level of quality acceptable for internal control in the federal government states that information should be recorded within a time frame that enables management to carry out responsibilities, and that operational information is needed in part to

---

[73]The Intelligence Authorization Act for Fiscal Year 2010, Pub. L. No. 111-259, § 367 (2010) (codified in relevant part at 50 U.S.C. § 3104),

determine whether the agency is complying with applicable laws and regulations.[74]

When we compared the number of employees eligible to access classified information in fiscal year 2013[75] as reported in JPAS to the total number of employees who served or worked in DOD[76] for that same fiscal year, we found that the number of DOD employees who were eligible to access classified information exceeded the total number of DOD employees in five components. As shown in table 4, the number of employees eligible to access classified information exceeded the total number of employees in the following groups: Air Force active-duty military and federal civilian personnel, Navy active-duty military and federal civilian personnel, and Marine Corps active-duty military personnel. However, Executive Order 12968 provides that the number of employees that each agency determines is eligible for access to classified information shall be kept to the minimum required for conduct of agency functions.

---

[74]GAO, *Standards for Internal Control in the Federal Government*, GAO/AIMD-00-21.3.1 (Nov. 1999), pp. 18, 19.

[75]The number of employees eligible to access classified information was obtained from JPAS, and includes all employees who had an active or valid confidential, secret, top secret, or sensitive compartmented information eligibility at the end of fiscal year 2013, and who did not have a separation date recorded in JPAS prior to the end of the fiscal year.

[76]To determine the total number of active-duty, reserve, and federal civilian employees in each component during fiscal year 2013, DMDC added the totals of all personnel who were employed during each month in fiscal year 2013. To avoid double-counting, personnel whose Social Security number had already been included in a prior month's report were removed from each service's monthly totals.

Table 4: Comparison of DOD Personnel with Clearance Eligibility and DOD Total Employees by Component for Fiscal Year 2013

Component	Employee type	Total employees eligible to access classified information[a]	Total personnel[c]	Percentage of employees with eligibility
Air Force	Civilian	225,269	187,207	120%
	Military—Active	551,127	356,982	154
	Military—Reserves[b]	154,712	310,418	50
Army	Civilian	296,481	300,098	99
	Military—Active	563,694	624,392	90
	Military—Reserves[b]	268,086	867,344	31
Marine Corps	Civilian	7,542	21,675	35
	Military—Active	355,030	229,537	155
	Military—Reserves[b]	40,329	134,395	30
Navy	Civilian	237,191	189,444	125
	Military—Active	356,153	355,453	100+
	Military—Reserves[b]	81,512	166,813	49
DOD Military Services Total	All personnel total	3,137,126	3,743,758	84%
Washington Headquarters Services[d]	Civilian	131,877	Unavailable[e]	
	Military	209		
	All personnel total	132,086		
Industry	Contractors government-wide	930,446	Unknown[f]	

Source: GAO analysis of Defense Manpower Data Center data. | GAO-14-460

[a]Total persons eligible to access classified information includes all employees without a separation date recorded in the Joint Personnel Adjudication System (JPAS) by the end of fiscal year 2013, who had eligibility for confidential, secret, top-secret, and SCI-level personnel security clearances. If a person had eligibility in more than one employee type, persons were only counted once, using the following ranking: (1) industry, (2) civilian, (3) active military, and (4) reserve military. We believe that these numbers are inaccurate.

[b]Reserve data includes counts for all Reserve component categories (Ready Reserve, Standby Reserve, and Retired Reserve), including the National Guard.

[c]Total personnel is the number of employees who, at any time during the fiscal year, served as a part-time or full-time federal civilian employee, served in an active component, or served in a reserve component. The totals for each group were calculated by adding the totals from 12 monthly files for fiscal year 2013 from the Appropriated Fund Civilians, Automated Extract of Active Duty Military Personnel Records, and the Reserve Components Common Personnel Data System databases, and then dropping duplicate personnel based on Social Security number and service.

[d]Washington Headquarters Services provides human capital support and manages the personnel security process for several DOD components and agencies.

[e]The total personnel data for the Washington Headquarters Services and other defense agencies did not include personnel for five organizations that were included in the JPAS eligibility data.

ʰThe total number of contractor employees working for the federal government is unknown, because agencies often contract for a service to be performed rather than for a specified number of individuals. In May 2014, we reported that DOD, the federal government's largest purchaser of contractor-provided services, reported having an estimated 670,000 contractor full-time equivalent employees in fiscal year 2012. See GAO, *Defense Acquisitions: Update on DOD's Efforts to Implement a Common Contractor Manpower Data System*, GAO-14-491R (May 19, 2014), and *Human Capital: Additional Steps Needed to Help Determine the Right Size and Composition of DOD's Total Workforce*, GAO-13-470 (May 29, 2013).

When we asked DMDC officials for their opinions on why the number of employees eligible to access classified information was greater than the total number of employees for some of the DOD components, they provided some possible explanations for the discrepancy. For example, DMDC officials explained that the database includes individuals who have newly enlisted into the military services but who may not have begun their enlistment period yet, and this would not be included in the employee totals. However, we reviewed data reported by the Under Secretary of Defense for Personnel and Readiness for fiscal years 2010 through 2012, and found that the total number of all personnel who joined each year (not just those who joined with a delayed entry date) each year ranged from about 43,000 to 44,000 for the Air Force and around 40,000 to 42,000 for the Marine Corps,[77] which is too few to explain the discrepancy of almost 200,000 for Air Force military personnel and 125,000 for Marine Corps military personnel.

Furthermore, DOD officials said that the information in JPAS may not reflect changes in personnel status such as separations due to retirements, employee job transfers, and deaths. DMDC officials explained that JPAS receives data from the components' personnel centers, and DMDC is dependent on the components to send separation information. As a result, the number of DOD clearance holders included in the report to Congress likely overstates the total number of DOD employees eligible to access classified information because it may include people whose clearance eligibility has not yet expired, but who have separated from the department, since JPAS was not updated to reflect that separation information. ODNI officials stated that because DOD has the largest number of eligible persons in the federal government, any overstatement of DOD's data will have a greater effect on the reported totals than for other agencies.

---

[77]These figures include both enlisted and officer accessions for the active and reserve components. Office of the Under Secretary of Defense, Personnel and Readiness, *Population Representation in the Military Services: Fiscal Year 2012 Summary Report*.

DMDC officials stated that since management of JPAS transitioned to DMDC in June 2010, DOD has conducted an extensive study on the quality of JPAS data. Specifically, they stated that DMDC has conducted more than 127 data-quality initiatives affecting 165 million records. These initiatives include examining records where the access level did not match the eligibility level (such as where a person has top-secret access but only secret eligibility) and identifying duplicate records. In addition, a DMDC official said that the team working on the migration from JPAS to the new system has identified data-quality issues that they are working to resolve.

Until DOD takes steps to review and analyze the discrepancies in the total number of employees and the number of employees eligible to access classified information, and address any problems identified, DOD will be unable to rely on the information provided by JPAS to get an accurate understanding of the total number of DOD employees eligible to access classified information. The lack of visibility over this total will impede the department's ability to implement recommendations to improve the security clearance process. For example, the February 2014 OMB report on the security, suitability, and credentialing processes recommended that federal agencies reduce the total population of clearance holders to minimize risk and reduce costs.[78] However, until DOD has an accurate baseline of the number of clearance holders in the department, DOD will be unable to determine the extent that it can or has reduced the number of clearance holders in accordance with this recommendation. Furthermore, having inaccurate data about the number of clearance holders within DOD will hinder the department's ability to provide oversight and accurate, complete information about security clearance eligibility to Congress as required by statute, to other offices within the department, and to interagency stakeholders.

Conclusions

In an environment where reciprocity of personnel security clearances is required among federal agencies, the consistent and transparent application of the processes governing whether individuals should retain their access to classified information has become increasingly important, so that all agencies can have reasonable assurance that only trustworthy individuals obtain and keep security clearances. Moreover, with the proposed implementation of continuous evaluation, the workload of

---

[78]Office of Management and Budget, *Suitability and Security Processes Review: Report to the President*.

agencies' security offices could significantly increase, making it critical for agencies to have a high-quality clearance revocation process in place. In the absence of requirements to track or report security clearance eligibility data and related metrics, DHS and DOD do not have key revocation data, such as the number of proposed revocations, to help oversee the revocation process or determine their workload for planning purposes.

Although both DHS and DOD are generally meeting their responsibilities and providing information to employees about most of their rights under the two executive orders governing the revocation process, until Army, Navy, and Coast Guard guidance is updated, some employees could potentially be denied some of the protections provided in the executive orders. Additionally, given the different interpretations of the executive order and other obstacles to implementation of the Secretary of Defense's direction to consolidate DOD's PSABs, in the absence of a resolution of these issues by the DOD General Counsel, DOD will be unable to implement the Secretary of Defense's direction to eliminate the overlap in this function.

Further, DHS, DOD, and some of their components have implemented the requirements from the executive orders in different ways. Without consistent processes for all employees, regardless of which component they work for, employees within DHS may experience different opportunities to cross-examine witnesses during the revocation process. In addition, without performance measures to assess the quality of the personnel security clearance revocation process, the ODNI, DHS, and DOD lack information to identify and resolve potential problems in the process, and make informed decisions about potential changes to the program. Further, until the DNI, as the Security Executive Agent, reviews the efficiency and effectiveness of the existing revocation processes, it is unknown whether having different processes, for military and civilian personnel and for contractors, and having inconsistencies among DHS and DOD, is the most appropriate approach to meet national security needs. Finally, without specific guidance from DHS and DOD on what information should be shared between personnel security and human capital offices, and when that information should be shared, DHS and DOD cannot ensure that individuals are treated in a fair and consistent manner. Similarly situated individuals who lose their security clearance may lose their employment or remain employed and be reassigned, based on their supervisor's discretion.

Moreover, without accurate data about the number of current DOD military and federal civilian employees eligible to access classified information, DOD is not well positioned to provide the information Congress has requested. DOD also will be hindered in implementing recommendations to reduce the total population of clearance holders in order to minimize risk and reduce cost.

Recommendations for Executive Action

We recommend that the Secretaries of Defense and Homeland Security, and the Director of National Intelligence take the following 13 actions.

To help ensure that the respective DHS and DOD data systems contain sufficiently complete and accurate information to facilitate effective oversight of the personnel security clearance revocation and appeal process, we recommend that

- the Secretary of Homeland Security direct the Chief Security Officer to assess the benefits and associated costs of tracking additional revocation and appeals information, and take any steps necessary to modify the Integrated Security Management System (ISMS) to track such information as is deemed beneficial; and

- the Secretary of Defense direct the Under Secretary of Defense for Intelligence to take steps to ensure that data are recorded and updated in the Joint Personnel Adjudication System (JPAS) and the department's new systems, so that the relevant fields are filled.

To help ensure that all employees within DHS receive the same protections during their personal appearance, we recommend that the Secretary of Homeland Security direct the Chief Security Officer to revise and finalize the DHS instruction regarding the personnel security program to clarify whether or not employees are allowed to cross-examine witnesses during personal appearances.

To help ensure independence and the efficient use of resources, we recommend that the Secretary of Defense direct the DOD General Counsel to take the following two actions:

- first, resolve the disagreement about the legal authority to consolidate the PSABs and, in collaboration with the PSABs and the Under Secretary of Defense for Intelligence, address any other obstacles to consolidating DOD's PSABs; and

- second, if the General Counsel determines that there are no legal impediments and that other obstacles to consolidation can be addressed, we recommend that the Secretary of Defense direct the Defense Legal Services Agency to take steps to implement the Secretary of Defense's direction to consolidate DOD's PSABs.

To help ensure that all employees within DOD receive the same rights during the revocation process, we recommend that the Secretary of Defense

- direct the Secretary of the Navy to revise Secretary of the Navy Manual M-5510.30 to specify that any information collected by the Navy PSAB from the employee's command will be shared with the employee, who will also be given the opportunity to respond to any such information provided; and

- direct the Secretary of the Army to revise Army Regulation 380-67 to specify that any information collected by the Army PSAB from the employee's command or by the Army PSAB itself will be shared with the employee, who will also be given the opportunity to respond to any such information provided.

To help ensure that all employees are treated fairly and receive the protections established in the executive order, we recommend that the Secretary of Homeland Security direct the Commandant, U.S. Coast Guard, to revise the Coast Guard instruction for military personnel to specify that military personnel may be represented by counsel or other representatives at their own expense.

To facilitate department-wide review and assessment of the quality of the personnel security clearance revocation process, we recommend that the DNI, in consultation with the Secretaries of Defense and Homeland Security, develop performance measures to better enable them to identify and resolve problems, and direct the collection of related revocation and appeals information.

To help ensure that similarly situated individuals are treated consistently, and to facilitate oversight and help ensure the quality of the security clearance revocation process, we recommend that the DNI review whether the existing security clearance revocation process is the most efficient and effective approach. In this review, the DNI should consider whether there should be a single personnel security clearance revocation process used across all executive-branch agencies and workforces, with consideration of areas such as the timing of the personal appearance in the revocation process, and the ability to cross-examine witnesses.

Further, to the extent that a single process or changes to the existing parallel processes are warranted, the DNI should consider whether there is a need to establish any policies and procedures to facilitate a more consistent process, and recommend as needed any revisions to existing executive orders or other executive-branch guidance.

To facilitate coordination between personnel security and human capital offices regarding how a security clearance revocation should affect an employee's employment status, and to help ensure that individuals are treated in a fair and consistent manner, we recommend that

- the Secretary of Homeland Security direct the Under Secretary for Management to review and revise policy regarding coordination between the personnel security and human capital offices to clarify what information can and should be communicated between human capital and personnel security officials at specified decision points in the revocation process, and when that information should be communicated; and

- the Secretary of Defense direct the Under Secretary of Defense for Personnel and Readiness, in consultation with the Under Secretary of Defense for Intelligence, to review and revise policy regarding coordination between the personnel security and human capital offices to clarify what information can and should be communicated between human capital and personnel security officials at specified decision points in the revocation process, and when that information should be communicated.

To help ensure that the DNI report to Congress contains accurate data about the number of current DOD military and federal civilian employees eligible to access classified information, we recommend that the Secretary of Defense direct the Under Secretary of Defense for Intelligence and the Under Secretary of Defense for Personnel and Readiness to review and analyze the discrepancies in the total number of employees and the number of employees eligible to access classified information, and take immediate steps to address the problems.

Agency Comments and Our Evaluation

We provided a draft of this report to DHS, DOD, and ODNI for review and comment. Written comments from DHS, DOD, and ODNI are reprinted in their entirety in appendices II, III, and IV respectively. All three agencies generally concurred with our recommendations and provided additional

GAO-14-640 Security Clearance Revocations

technical comments, which we incorporated in the report where appropriate.

In its written comments, DHS concurred with our four recommendations directed to it, and stated it has already taken steps to implement two of our recommendations.

- First, regarding our recommendation to assess the benefits and associated costs of tracking additional revocation and appeals information, DHS concurred, stating that the Office of the Chief Security Officer has established an estimated completion date of December 2014 to conduct a review to consider what additional data would be valuable for collection.

- Second, with respect to our recommendation to revise and finalize the DHS instruction regarding cross-examination of witnesses, DHS concurred, commenting that the Office of the Chief Security Officer has revised its personnel security instruction with unambiguous language on cross-examination of witnesses, and intends to issue the revised instruction by the end of the year.

- Third, for our recommendation to revise the Coast Guard instruction to specify that military personnel may be represented by counsel, DHS concurred, stating that the Coast Guard, pending the update of the Commandant Instruction on Personnel Security, issued an interim memorandum in May 2014 advising that individuals may have counsel or other representatives present at the second-level review at their own expense. DHS also stated that it believes the Coast Guard's actions to implement our recommendation regarding the revision of its instruction to specify that military personnel may be represented by counsel fulfill the intent of the recommendation, and requested that this recommendation be closed as implemented. While we are encouraged by the actions the Coast Guard has already taken, we continue to believe that it is important that the change be formalized in the updated Commandant instruction before we close out our recommendation. Moreover, the revision made by the Coast Guard in its interim memorandum appears to extend the right to counsel only to the personal appearance, and does not make clear how employees will be informed of their right to counsel, but under Executive Order 12968 the right to counsel is not limited to one specific stage of the revocation process, and the order requires that employees be informed of this right.

- Finally, regarding our recommendation to review and revise policy regarding coordination between the personnel security and human capital offices, DHS concurred, commenting that the DHS Office of the Chief Human Capital Officer concurs with the concept of facilitating coordination between the personnel security and human capital offices, and will assess the process to determine appropriate communication points and provide appropriate guidance. DHS established an estimated completion date of March 2015 for this action. Further, in its technical comments, DHS noted that this recommendation would be more appropriately directed to the DHS Under Secretary for Management, who oversees both the Office of the Chief Human Capital Officer and the Office of the Chief Security Officer. As a result, we have modified the recipient of this recommendation as suggested.

In its written comments, DOD fully concurred with all but one of our seven recommendations directed to it, and partially concurred with one of our recommendations.

- First, with respect to our recommendation to ensure data are recorded and updated in JPAS and DOD's new systems, DOD concurred, stating that the Office of the Under Secretary of Defense for Intelligence will incorporate monitoring of data fields pertaining to the personnel security clearance revocation and appeal process into its quarterly oversight of DOD Personnel Security Program metrics.

- Regarding our two recommendations to revise Navy and Army guidance, respectively, about sharing information collected by the respective PSABs with the employee, DOD concurred with both recommendations. DOD commented that the Navy plans to issue interim guidance by October 1, 2014, and issue the final revised Navy Manual by October 1, 2015. DOD further stated that the Army Regulation is under revision and will specify that the PSAB will provide any documents it obtains to the subject and allow a period of time for response.

- With respect to our recommendation to review and revise policy regarding coordination between the personnel security and human capital offices, DOD concurred, stating that the Office of the Under Secretary of Defense for Personnel and Readiness, with support from the Office of the Under Secretary of Defense for Intelligence, will identify the way forward to review and revise policy and procedures regarding coordination between the personnel security and human capital offices as appropriate.

- Finally, regarding our recommendation to review and analyze the discrepancies in the total number of employees and the number of employees eligible to access classified information, DOD concurred, commenting that within 30 days of the release of the final report, the Office of the Under Secretary of Defense for Intelligence will convene a meeting of action officers and analysts to identify strategies for reviewing, analyzing, and resolving the discrepancies in the total number of employees and the number of employees eligible to access classified information.

DOD partially concurred with our draft recommendation for the DOD General Counsel to resolve the disagreement about the legal authority to consolidate the PSABs and address any other obstacles to consolidation, and to implement the Secretary of Defense's direction to consolidate DOD's PSABs if there are no legal or other impediments to consolidation. DOD agreed with us to review legal or other impediments to consolidation, and stated that the DOD Office of General Counsel will address any unresolved disagreements about legal authority for consolidation of PSABs. DOD further commented that the DOD Office of General Counsel will work closely with the Office of the Under Secretary of Defense for Intelligence to address other issues concerning consolidation of PSABs. However, DOD commented that some DOD components disagreed with PSAB consolidation. Specifically, DOD stated that of the eleven components that provided responses to the draft report, eight concurred or had no issues or comments, while the remaining three components noted that the PSABs should remain at the component level and not be consolidated. One of these three components also commented that the perceived efficiencies from consolidation described in our report should be validated and that all models for consolidation should be evaluated before a decision is made that would consolidate the PSABs. DOD's comments reflect internal disagreement, which corroborates our finding that there is disagreement within DOD on the legal authority, risks, and benefits of consolidating the department's multiple appeals boards. As we also note in our report, the Secretary of Defense has already directed this consolidation. However, in light of statements from some DOD officials that DOD needs to study the implications of moving to a consolidated appeal board to make an informed decision, we clarified our recommendation to clearly separate the two actions to be taken by the DOD General Counsel: first to resolve the disagreement about the legal authority for consolidation and address other obstacles, and second to take steps to implement the consolidation if there are no legal impediments and the other obstacles to consolidation can be addressed. We believe this language addresses the need for DOD to fully consider and resolve the components' concerns about consolidation.

In its written comments, ODNI concurred with our two recommendations directed to it, for ODNI to develop performance measures and direct the collection of related revocation and appeals information, and to review whether the existing security clearance revocation process is the most efficient and effective approach. ODNI stated it established the Security Executive Agent National Assessment Program in April 2014 to conduct oversight of personnel security processes across the Executive Branch. ODNI said that this program includes gathering and analyzing data to establish standard processes as appropriate and developing performance measures against those standards. ODNI further commented that DHS and DOD have implemented revocation processes in different ways, which warrant additional ODNI oversight of agency revocation policies. DOD also concurred with our recommendation directed to ODNI regarding development of performance measures and collection of related revocation and appeals information, stating that the Office of the Under Secretary of Defense for Intelligence would ensure that ODNI receives a copy and is made aware of this recommendation.

We are sending copies of this report to appropriate congressional committees, the Secretaries of Homeland Security and Defense, and the DNI. The report also is available at no charge on the GAO website at http://www.gao.gov.

If you or your staff have any questions about this report, please contact me at (202) 512-3604 or farrellb@gao.gov. Contact points for our Offices of Congressional Relations and Public Affairs may be found on the last page of this report. GAO staff who made key contributions to this report are listed in appendix V.

Sincerely yours,

Brenda S. Farrell
Director, Defense Capabilities and Management

GAO-14-640 Security Clearance Revocations

Appendix I: Scope and Methodology

This report assesses the policies and practices that the Department of Homeland Security (DHS) and Department of Defense (DOD) use when revoking personnel security clearances. The scope of our work focused on the revocation of personnel security clearances for federal civilian employees and military personnel within DHS and DOD, as well as federal government contractors. Known intelligence community military and civilian personnel and contractors were excluded from our scope, because they follow different processes and guidance than other DOD personnel. Table 5 provides a complete list of the agencies we contacted for our review.

Table 5: Agencies Contacted during Review

Agency	Associated offices and components
Department of Homeland Security (DHS)	
	Office of the Chief Security Officer
	Office of the Chief Human Capital Officer
	Federal Emergency Management Agency
	Transportation Security Administration
	U.S. Citizenship and Immigration Services
	U.S. Coast Guard
	U.S. Customs and Border Protection
	U.S. Immigration and Customs Enforcement
	U.S. Secret Service
Department of Defense (DOD)	
	Office of Under Secretary of Defense for Intelligence
	Office of the Under Secretary of Defense for Personnel and Readiness
	Defense Office of Hearings and Appeals
	Defense Security Service
	Defense Manpower Data Center
	Consolidated Adjudications Facility
	Headquarters Department of the Army
	Army Personnel Security Appeals Board
	Assistant Secretary of the Navy
	Deputy Chief of Naval Operations
	Navy Personnel Security Appeals Board
	Headquarters Marine Corps

GAO-14-640 Security Clearance Revocations

Agency	Associated offices and components
	Headquarters Air Force
	Air Force Personnel Security Appeal Board
	Washington Headquarters Services
Office of the Director of National Intelligence (ODNI)	

Source: GAO.| GAO-14-640

To examine the extent to which DHS and DOD track data to oversee their revocation processes, and what these data show, we analyzed relevant executive orders and DHS and DOD personnel security clearance revocation policies to identify the extent to which they are required to maintain or report data and documentation on their security clearance revocation and appeals processes. We compared those requirements to leading practices, and assessed the extent that the policy requirements comply with these leading practices.[1] In addition, we requested and obtained DHS and DOD personnel security clearance revocation and appeal data.

Revocation data for DHS was provided by DHS's Office of the Chief Security Officer using its system for managing and standardizing personnel security processes and data, the Integrated Security Management System (ISMS). Personnel security records maintained in ISMS include suitability and security clearance investigations, which contain information related to background checks, investigations, and access determinations. The reported DHS security clearance revocation and appeals data include DHS military personnel and federal civilian employees within DHS Headquarters and the DHS operational components. DHS revocation cases for its contractor employees are processed by DOD and were not included in the DHS data. Although we requested data from fiscal years 2009 through 2013, DHS officials from Office of the Chief Security Officer could only provide revocation data for fiscal years 2011through 2013, because not all of the DHS operational components had been using ISMS to manage personnel and administrative security case records until recently. DHS Headquarters

---

[1]GAO, *Assessing the Reliability of Computer-Processed Data*, GAO-09-680G (Washington, D.C.: July 2009), and *Executive Guide: Effectively Implementing the Government Performance and Results Act*, GAO/GGD-96-118 (Washington, D.C.: June 1996).

migrated data from its legacy system into and began using ISMS in May 2008; Federal Emergency Management Agency migrated to ISMS in May 2009; U.S. Customs and Border Protection migrated in October 2009; U.S. Immigration and Customs Enforcement migrated in December 2009; U.S. Citizenship and Immigration Services migrated in December 2009; U.S. Coast Guard migrated in July 2011; Transportation Security Administration migrated in December 2012; and U.S. Secret Service migrated in May 2013.

To provide the revocation data we requested regarding the number of revocations and the reasons for the revocation under the adjudicative guidelines, DHS queried ISMS and then validated those results with each of its operational components. The components made changes to the ISMS data when they determined that the data entered into ISMS did not track with what they had tracked elsewhere. DHS officials said that the differences were likely based on data entry and system use issues. The total number of revocation cases and the total number of revocation cases that went to the Security Appeals Board represents DHS military and civilian employees' revocation cases that were closed in that particular fiscal year. We found that the total number of cases where a revocation proceeding was initiated could be higher because ISMS does not track cases where a person separated from the agency before a final decision was made on a proposal to revoke a personnel security clearance. In addition, the total number of military and civilian employees eligible to access classified information represents a current snapshot in time as ISMS does not track historical security clearance numbers. To corroborate the accuracy of the ISMS total number of DHS employees eligible to access classified information at each component, we compared this information to the total number of employees at six DHS components (U.S. Coast Guard, Transportation Security Administration, Federal Emergency Management Agency, U.S. Immigration and Customs Enforcement, U.S. Citizenship and Immigration Services, and U.S. Customs and Border Protection). We found that in all six components, the total number of employees was greater than the number of employees eligible to access classified information, as not all DHS employees need eligibility for access.

Furthermore, while we requested DHS data on the number of employees that filed an initial appeal and the average amount of time it takes to complete a revocation case, these data were not available. Officials from the Office of the Chief Security Officer told us that ISMS has a module, called the Appeals Case, that could provide information about the number of initial appeals, but because use of this module is not required, only a few DHS components use it. Furthermore, officials from the Office of the Chief Security Officer told us that ISMS cannot track case timeliness data as a whole across the DHS components, because each appeal level would be saved as a different appeals case module entry, but the officials explained that they could determine this information for a particular case by looking at the individual ISMS records. We analyzed the DHS revocation data and supporting documentation, and discussed its reliability with DHS officials, and found the data to be sufficiently reliable to report on the number of employees whose personnel security clearance was revoked in DHS, and the reasons for the revocations.

Revocation data for DOD military and federal civilian personnel and for industry or contractor personnel government-wide was provided by the Defense Manpower Data Center from DOD's Joint Personnel Adjudication System (JPAS), which is DOD's system of record for personnel security management to record and document personnel security actions. DOD security clearance revocation and appeals data include military personnel and federal civilian employees within the military services (Army, Navy, Air Force, and Marine Corps) and the defense agencies (referred to as Washington Headquarters Services). Data for government-wide contractors (also referred as industry personnel) is collectively grouped as one entity because Defense Manpower Data Center officials informed us that data on contractor personnel do not indicate the agency with which an individual's contract is associated. We met with officials from the Office of the Under Secretary of Defense for Intelligence and the Defense Manpower Data Center (the administrator of JPAS) to discuss the approach for our data request and to get their feedback. We requested JPAS data extracts showing the total number of persons eligible to access classified information, the number of security clearance revocations, the reasons for a revocation decision, the number of appeals, the number of favorable and unfavorable appeal decisions, the type of appeal selected by the individual (personal appearance or in writing), and the time values at different intervals of the revocation and appeal process. We requested that all of these data be broken out by each DOD component for DOD military personnel, DOD federal civilian employees, and government-wide contractor employees for fiscal years 2009 through 2013.

Furthermore, while we requested DOD data on the number of employees that filed an appeal, appeal outcomes, and the average amount of time it takes to complete a revocation case, these data were not available. Although there are fields in JPAS where this information can be recorded, we found that these fields were not consistently being used in JPAS.

Defense Manpower Data Center officials initially provided mock-ups of the data request that excluded these data fields or left them blank. When we asked about this, Defense Manpower Data Center officials stated that it is their agency's practice not to provide information from data fields with less than 50 percent fill rates. We asked that Defense Manpower Data Center to provide all the requested data along with an additional worksheet to show the data fill rate percentage, so we could report on the extent that these data fields had not been used.

To corroborate the accuracy of the JPAS revocation data for DOD military and civilian employees, we asked DOD officials from the DOD Consolidated Adjudications Facility (CAF) to provide us with the number of revocations processed by their adjudicators for the military departments' military and civilian employees for fiscal years 2009 through 2013. We compared the JPAS data received from Defense Manpower Data Center with the data provided by the DOD CAF and we found that the data did not match. We determined that the discrepancy with the DOD CAF data was likely caused by a difference in the periods and populations included in the counts.

To corroborate the accuracy of the JPAS revocation data for contractor personnel, and data regarding the personal appearance for DOD military and civilian employees, we asked DOD officials from Defense Office of Hearings and Appeals (DOHA) to provide information on the number of contractor hearings and appeals performed, and their outcomes, for fiscal years 2009 through 2013 and the number of personal appearances for DOD military and civilian employees and their outcomes for fiscal years 2009 through 2013. We compared the JPAS data received from the Defense Manpower Data Center with the data provided by DOHA and we found that the data did not match. We determined that the discrepancy with the contractor data from DOHA was a result of the inclusion of clearance denials, which the DOHA database was unable to separate from clearance revocations. Security clearance denials were not part of the scope of this review. We analyzed the DOD revocation data and supporting documentation, and discussed their reliability with DOD officials, and found the data to be sufficiently reliable to report on the number of military personnel and federal civilian employees and contractors whose personnel security clearances were revoked in DOD, and the reasons for the revocations.

To examine the extent to which DHS and DOD consistently implemented government-wide requirements in their revocation processes, we obtained and reviewed the policies and procedures DHS, DOD, and their components use when revoking an employee's access to classified information, interviewed DHS and DOD officials about whether these processes are being uniformly applied within each department and across the departments, and discussed the officials' suggestions for improving the revocation process. In addition, we reviewed Executive Orders 12968 and 10865, which establish the overall process for revoking an employee's security clearance, to identify agency and employee rights and responsibilities during the clearance revocation process. We then analyzed DHS and DOD template or redacted sample communication letters sent to employees during the revocation and appeal process by each component within DHS and DOD to determine whether they provide employees notice of their security clearance revocation rights and responsibilities under Executive Orders 12968 and 10865. Two analysts independently reviewed and assessed the DHS and DOD communication letters to determine whether they contain the 14 key rights and responsibilities for military, civilian, and contractor employees provided by Executive Order 12968 and the three additional rights for contractor employees provided by Executive Order 10865.[2] For DHS military and civilian employees, we reviewed the Notice of Determination, the Notice of Review, and the Security Appeals Board decision letter. For DOD military and civilian employees, we reviewed the Statement of Reasons, the Letter of Revocation, and the PSAB decision letter. For contractor employees government-wide, we reviewed a Statement of Reasons, the administrative judge's decision letter, and the DOHA Appeal Board decision letter. The analysts then compared their results to identify any disagreements and reached agreement on all items through discussion. We reviewed processes for civilian and military personnel within DHS and DOD, excluding the intelligence community, and for industry or contractor personnel that are part of the 23 executive-branch agencies that follow the DOD guidance and process.

Additionally, we interviewed officials from DHS, DOD, and their respective components to discuss (1) how they are following their policies, (2) how employee rights and responsibilities factor into the security clearance revocations process, and (3) how and under what circumstances they communicate with employees who are subject to the security clearance revocation process. When we identified discrepancies in following policies

---

[2]Executive Order No. 12968, *Access to Classified Information* (Aug. 2, 1995, as amended); Executive Order No. 10865, *Safeguarding Classified Information Within Industry* (Feb. 20, 1960, as amended).

or communicating with employees, we contacted appropriate DHS and DOD officials to determine the reasons for such discrepancies and their potential effect. We also met with DHS, DOD, and ODNI officials to discuss the oversight they provide over executive-branch agencies' personnel security revocation processes, their suggestions for building quality into the revocation process, and whether there are currently any metrics or reporting requirements related to personnel security clearance revocations.

To examine the extent to which DHS's and DOD's respective human capital and personnel security clearance revocation policies enable the departments to determine the employment status of their federal civilian and military employees subject to revocation in a consistent manner, we analyzed department-level and component level DHS and DOD human capital guidance—specifically their respective guidance for misconduct, discipline, and adverse actions, such as a table of penalties[3]—and personnel security guidance. We assessed the extent that this guidance could be used to systematically determine what actions the agencies should take regarding the employment status of individuals subject to the clearance revocation and appeals processes, and what employment actions, such as reassignment or separation, are typically taken if an employee's personnel security clearance is revoked. In addition, we assessed the extent to which the different sources of guidance are linked or are cross-referenced, and assessed what communication is required to take place between an agency's personnel security office and human capital office during the course of a clearance revocation proceeding. We also interviewed human capital officials at DHS, DOD, and their components to obtain their perspectives on the extent that DHS and DOD's human capital practices regarding the employment status of individuals subject to revocation are linked to and aligned with personnel security policies related to security clearance revocation, and the extent that there is communication between an agency's personnel security office and a human capital office during the course of a clearance revocation proceeding.

In addition, we analyzed DHS's, DOD's, and the components' guidance to determine whether the departments required tracking of any data

---

[3]A table of penalties establishes an appropriate range of punishment for an offense, and also may identify mitigating and exacerbating factors that a commander or supervisor should consider in making decisions.

regarding the employment outcomes of individuals whose personnel security clearances were revoked. We also discussed with DHS and DOD officials what data regarding employment outcomes were available at the department and component level. For this objective, within DHS, we focused on the three DHS components that had the largest number of personnel security clearance revocations from fiscal years 2011 through 2013, which were the U.S. Coast Guard, U.S. Immigration and Customs Enforcement, and U.S. Secret Service. Within DOD, our review included the headquarters-level elements of the Departments of the Army, the Navy, and the Air Force; the Marine Corps, and the Washington Headquarters Services. Contractor personnel were not included in the scope of this objective, as the human capital policies applicable to contractors would be those of their private-sector employers.

To assess whether DOD's personnel security management system accurately reports the total number of DOD employees eligible for access to classified information, we compared the total number of DOD employees eligible for access to classified information reported by DOD's personnel security management system to the total number of DOD employees in each component. To corroborate the accuracy of the JPAS total number of military and federal civilian employees eligible to access classified information, we compared this information with total military personnel end strength and civilian personnel full-time equivalents from the Under Secretary of Defense Comptroller's National Defense Budget Estimates (Green Book). We assumed that the total number of military and civilian employees in each component should be higher than the total number of military and civilian employees who were eligible to access classified information, because not all DOD employees should be required to have clearance eligibility. However, we found that the total number of military and civilian employees eligible to access classified information in fiscal year 2013 as reported by JPAS was higher than the total number of military and civilian employees listed in the fiscal 2013 military personnel end strength and civilian personnel full-time equivalent data found in the DOD Green Book. We met with officials from Defense Manpower Data Center to discuss the discrepancies. Regarding the disparity in the revocation data, the Defense Manpower Data Center officials stated that they could not speak for the accuracy of the data derived from the Green Book, since full-time equivalents would undercount the total number of individuals employed, due to issues such as two part-time individuals occupying one full-time position. As a result, they believed that it would not be appropriate to compare these data against the total number of persons eligible to access classified information. DMDC officials subsequently agreed to provide us with counts for the total numbers of DOD active-duty and reserve military personnel and federal civilian employees for fiscal year 2013.

To determine the total number of DOD active-duty military personnel who were employed at any time in each active component during fiscal year 2013, data were taken from the Automated Extract of Active Duty Military Personnel Records. DMDC calculated the total number of active-duty military personnel by adding the totals from all 12 monthly files for fiscal year 2013 that were counted and reported as part of official active component strength.[4] After combining the 12 files, duplicate personnel were dropped based on Social Security number and service. This methodology could potentially double-count individuals if someone transferred from one active service to another active service (e.g., if an individual transferred from active duty in the Army to active duty in the Navy).

To determine the total number of DOD reserve personnel who were employed at any time in each component during fiscal year 2013, data for reserve personnel were taken from the Reserve Components Common Personnel Data System. Reserve personnel data includes all Reserve categories in the Reserve and National Guard (Ready Reserve, Standby Reserve, and Retired Reserve). DMDC calculated the total number of reserve personnel by adding the totals of all members of the reserve components from all 12 monthly files for fiscal year 2013.[5] After combining the 12 files, duplicate personnel were dropped based on Social Security number and service.

To determine the total number of DOD federal civilian employees who were employed at any time in each component during fiscal year 2013, data for federal civilian personnel were taken from the Appropriated Fund Civilians data files. DMDC calculated the total number of federal civilian employees by adding the totals from all 12 monthly files for fiscal year 2013 that were counted and reported on direct-hire civilians paid exclusively from DOD appropriated funds, which includes full-time

---

[4]This count includes strength and nonstrength accountable personnel, such as prisoners of war, missing personnel, deserters, prisoners in civil or military confinement for 6 months or more, and personnel on appellate leave (with or without pay).

[5]This count excludes reserve personnel who were counted within the active end strengths of the components, which is usually those who serve on active duty for more than 180 days.

GAO-14-640 Security Clearance Revocations

permanent and non-full-time permanent employees.[6] After combining the 12 files, duplicate personnel were dropped based on Social Security number and service. This methodology could potentially double-count individuals if someone transferred from one agency to another agency (e.g., if an individual transferred from an Army civilian position to a Navy civilian position).

Using these total employee counts, we still found that the number of DOD employees who were eligible to access classified information in five components exceeded the actual number of DOD employees in those components. Regarding the disparity in the revocation data, Defense Manpower Data Center officials stated that JPAS completeness and accuracy of the data is dependent on the users entering the data. They further stated that information in JPAS may not reflect the loss of personnel—due to changes such as retirements, employee job transfer, and deaths—in the different agencies in DOD, because the department's personnel centers can only send in separation dates for their personnel for a limited period and the personnel centers may not enter or correct an employee's status during this period. As a result, we did not find the JPAS data on the number of current military personnel and federal civilian employees and contractors who are eligible to access classified information to be reliable.

We conducted this performance audit from April 2013 to September 2014 in accordance with generally accepted government auditing standards. Those standards require that we plan and perform the audit to obtain sufficient, appropriate evidence to provide a reasonable basis for our findings and conclusions based on our audit objectives. We believe that the evidence obtained provides a reasonable basis for our findings and conclusions based on our audit objectives.

---

[6]This count includes civilian personnel who are U.S. citizens in U.S. and non-U.S. duty locations, non-U.S. citizens in U.S. duty locations, and military technicians.

Appendix II: Comments from the Department of Homeland Security

U.S. Department of Homeland Security
Washington, DC 20528

August 5, 2014

Brenda S. Farrell
Director, Defense Capabilities and Management
U.S. Government Accountability Office
441 G Street, NW
Washington, DC 20548

Re: Draft Report GAO-14-640, "PERSONNEL SECURITY CLEARANCES: Additional
        Guidance and Oversight Needed at DHS and DOD to Ensure Consistent Application of
        Revocation Process"

Dear Ms. Farrell:

Thank you for the opportunity to review and comment on this draft report. The U.S. Department of
Homeland Security (DHS) appreciates the U.S. Government Accountability Office's (GAO's) work
in planning and conducting its review and issuing this report.

DHS is pleased to note GAO's recognition that the Department has taken steps to improve the
quality of the security clearance revocation process. DHS appreciates GAO's detailed discussion of
the revocation process and understands the importance of establishing guidance and oversight of
such processes. In particular, DHS notes GAO's responsiveness to agency comments throughout the
audit and commends its attention to detail in capturing the nuance and challenges inherent to
personnel security. DHS remains committed to continuing to improve its personnel security
processes and procedures.

The draft report contained four recommendations for DHS, with which the Department concurs.
Specifically, GAO recommended that the Secretary of Homeland Security:

Recommendation 1: Direct the Chief Security Officer to assess the benefits and associated costs of
tracking additional revocation and appeals information, and take any steps necessary to modify
ISMS to track such information as is deemed beneficial.

Response: Concur. The DHS Office of the Chief Security Officer (OCSO) uses the Integrated
Security Management System (ISMS) to track specific information on security clearance revocations
and appeals. OCSO will conduct a review to consider what additional data would be valuable for
collection as well as the technical and usage requirements of such a change. Estimated Completion
Date (ECD): December 31, 2014.

Recommendation 2: Direct the Chief Security Officer to revise and finalize its instruction to clarify whether or not employees are allowed to cross-examine witnesses during the personal appearance.

Response: Concur. OCSO has revised its personnel security instruction with unambiguous language on cross-examination of witnesses during the appeals process personal appearance. The instruction is in the final stages of review and will be issued by the end of the year. ECD: December 31, 2014.

Recommendation 3: Direct the Commandant, U.S. Coast Guard, to revise the U.S. Coast Guard Instruction for military personnel to specify that military personnel may be represented by counsel or other representative at their own expense.

Response: Concur. The U.S. Coast Guard has already taken steps to implement this recommendation. Effective 2013, the Deputy Commandant for Mission Support no longer restricts military personnel from employing legal counsel. Pending the update of Commandant Instruction 5520.12C on Personnel Security, this was communicated in an interim memorandum dated May 15, 2014, advising that "individuals may have counsel or other representative present at the second level review at the member's own expense. Members are responsible for providing a signed statement designating such representation, as consent to such presence." We believe these actions fulfill the intent of the recommendation and request that it be closed as implemented.

Recommendation 4: Direct the Chief Human Capital Officer, in consultation with the Chief Security Officer, to review and revise policy regarding coordination between the personnel security and human capital offices to clarify what information can and should be communicated between human capital and personnel security officials at specified decision points in the revocation process, and when that information should be communicated.

Response: Concur. The DHS Office of the Chief Human Capital Officer concurs with the concept of facilitating coordination between the personnel security and human capital offices and will assess the process to determine appropriate communication points and provide appropriate guidance. ECD: March 31, 2015.

Again, thank you for the opportunity to review and comment on this draft report. Technical comments were previously provided under separate cover. Please feel free to contact me if you have any questions. We look forward to working with you in the future.

Sincerely,

Jim H. Crumpacker, CIA, CFE
Director
Departmental GAO-OIG Liaison Office

2

Appendix III: Comments from the Department of Defense

UNDER SECRETARY OF DEFENSE
5000 DEFENSE PENTAGON
WASHINGTON, DC 20301-5000

AUG 2 0 2014

INTELLIGENCE

Ms. Brenda S. Farrell
Director
Defense Capabilities and Management
Government Accountability Office
Washington, DC 20548

Dear Ms. Farrell:

This is the Department of Defense (DoD) response to the Government Accountability Office (GAO) Draft Report, GAO-14-640, "PERSONNEL SECURITY CLEARANCES: Additional Guidance and Oversight Needed at DHS and DoD to Ensure Consistent Application of Revocation Process," dated July 9, 2014 (GAO Code 351813)." The enclosure provides the DoD responses to the specific recommendations in the report.

DoD components concurred or stated no issues with all but one of the recommendations of the report. The one exception pertained to consolidation of personnel security appeals boards (PSABs) within the DoD. While some DoD Components disagreed with PSAB consolidation, they did agree with – or did not object to – the GAO's recommendation for a review of legal or other impediments to consolidation.

My point of contact for this effort is Dr. Kelly Buck, (703) 604-1130 or kelly.r.buck2.civ@mail.mil.

Sincerely,

PDUSDI for

Michael G. Vickers

Attachments:
As stated

GAO DRAFT REPORT DATED JULY 9, 2014
GAO-14-640 (GAO CODE 351813)

"PERSONNEL SECURITY CLEARANCES: ADDITIONAL
GUIDANCE AND OVERSIGHT NEEDED AT DHS AND DOD
TO ENSURE CONSISTENT APPLICATION OF
REVOCATION PROCESS"

DEPARTMENT OF DEFENSE COMMENTS
TO THE GAO RECOMMENDATIONS

RECOMMENDATION 1: To help ensure that the DoD data systems contain
sufficiently complete and accurate information to facilitate effective oversight of the
personnel security clearance revocation and appeal process, GAO recommends that the
Secretary of Defense direct the Under Secretary of Defense (Intelligence) to take steps to
ensure that data is recorded and updated in JPAS and the department's new systems, so
that the relevant fields are filled.

> **DoD RESPONSE:** Concur. The Office of the Under Secretary of Defense for
> Intelligence (OUSD(I)) will incorporate monitoring of data fields pertaining to the
> personnel security clearance revocation and appeal process into its quarterly
> oversight of DoD Personnel Security Program metrics.

RECOMMENDATION 2: To help ensure independence and the efficient use of
resources, we recommend that the Secretary of Defense direct the DoD General Counsel
to resolve the disagreement about the legal authority to consolidate the PSABs and, in
collaboration with the PSABs and the Under Secretary of Defense for Intelligence,
address any other obstacles to consolidating DOD's PSABs. If the General Counsel
determines that there are no legal or other impediments to consolidation, GAO
recommends that that Secretary of Defense direct the Defense Legal Services Agency to
take steps to implement the Secretary of Defense's direction to consolidate DOD's
PSABs.

> **DoD RESPONSE:** Partially Concur. Of the eleven components that provided
> responses to the draft report, eight concurred or had no issues or comments. Of
> the remaining three Components, two respondents non-concurred, and one took a
> similar view. One non-concurred for the following reason: PSABs conducted
> under the authority of the Head of an Intelligence Community Element (HICE)
> should remain under the operation and control of that particular agency and not
> consolidated into a single PSAB. This component believes that
> consolidation would prevent the HICE from exercising its authority to render
> final eligibility determinations in support of unique mission requirements.
> Another response supported the recommended DoD General Counsel review of

2

authorities that govern the establishment of PSABs within DoD. They also stated, however, that even if such a review resulted in a conclusion that law and policy would not preclude the consolidation of DoD PSABs, this component would not support it because they believe their PSAB must maintain the authority to exercise this important risk-based determination. A third response noted that PSABs should remain at the component level, but also stated that the perceived efficiencies from consolidation described in the report should be validated and that all models for consolidation should be evaluated before a decision is made that would consolidate the PSAB within the Defense Office of Hearings and Appeals. All other coordinators, concurred with this recommendation as written or had no comments. The DoD Office of General Counsel will address any unresolved disagreements about legal authority for consolidation of PSABs and will work closely with USD(I) to address other issues concerning consolidation of PSABs.

RECOMMENDATION 3: To help ensure that all employees within DoD receive the same rights during the revocation process, we recommend that the Secretary of Defense direct the Secretary of the Navy to revise Secretary of the Navy Manual M-5510.30 to specify that any information collected by the Navy PSAB from the employee's command will be shared with the employee, who will also be given the opportunity to respond to any such information provided.

> **DoD RESPONSE**: Concur. The Navy plans to issue interim guidance by October 1, 2014. They expect to issue the final revised Navy Manual M-5510.30 by October 1, 2015.

RECOMMENDATION 4: To help ensure that all employees within DoD receive the same rights during the revocation process, we recommend that the Secretary of Defense direct the Secretary of the Army to revise Army Regulation 380-67 to specify that any information collected by the Army PSAB from the employee's command or by the Army PSAB itself will be shared with the employee, who will also be given the opportunity to respond to any such information provided.

> **DoD RESPONSE**: Concur. Army Regulation 380-67, Army Personnel Security Program, is under revision, and will specify that the PSAB will provide any documents it obtains after receipt of the personnel security file to the subject and allow the subject a period of time to respond to such information prior to rendering a PSAB decision.

RECOMMENDATION 5: GAO recommends that the Secretary of Defense take the following action: To facilitate department-wide review and assessment of the quality of the personnel security clearance revocation process, GAO recommends that the Director

3

of National Intelligence, in consultation with the Secretaries of Defense and Homeland Security, develop performance measures to better enable them to identify and resolve problems, and direct the collection of related revocation and appeals information.

> **DoD RESPONSE**: Concur. As soon as the GAO final report is released, the OUSD(I) will ensure that the Office of the Director of National Intelligence receives a copy and is made aware of this recommendation.

RECOMMENDATION 6: To facilitate coordination between personnel security and human capital offices regarding how a security clearance revocation should affect an employee's employment status, and to help ensure that individuals are treated in a fair and consistent manner, GAO recommends that the Secretary of Defense direct the Under Secretary of Defense for Personnel and Readiness, in consultation with the Under Secretary of Defense (Intelligence), to review and revise policy regarding coordination between the personnel security and human capital offices to clarify what information can and should be communicated between human capital and personnel security officials at specified decision points in the revocation process, and when that information should be communicated.

> **DoD RESPONSE**: Concur. Upon release of the final GAO report, OUSD(P&R), with OUSD(I)'s support, will identify the way forward for reviewing and revising policy and procedures, as appropriate, to ensure that individuals are treated in a fair and consistent manner.

RECOMMENDATION 7: To help ensure that the DNI report to Congress contains accurate data about the number of current DOD military and federal civilian employees eligible to access classified information, GAO recommends that the Secretary of Defense direct the Under Secretary of Defense (Intelligence) and the Under Secretary of Defense for Personnel and Readiness to review and analyze the discrepancies in the total number of employees and the number of employees eligible to access classified information, and take immediate steps to address the problems.

> **DoD RESPONSE**: Concur. Within 30 days of the release of the final GAO report, OUSD(I) will convene a meeting of action officers and analysts from both organizations to identify strategies for reviewing, analyzing, and resolving the discrepancies, as appropriate.

Appendix IV: Comments from the Office of the Director of National Intelligence

OFFICE OF THE DIRECTOR OF NATIONAL INTELLIGENCE
WASHINGTON, DC 20511

Ms. Brenda S. Farrell   AUG 08 2014
Director
Defense Capabilities and Management
U.S. Government Accountability Office
441 G Street, N.W.
Washington, D.C. 20548

Dear Ms. Farrell:

The Office of the Director of National Intelligence (ODNI) appreciates the opportunity to respond to the Government Accountability Office's (GAO) draft report, *Personnel Security Clearances: Additional Guidance and Oversight Needed at DHS and DOD to Ensure Consistent Application of Revocation Process* (GAO-14-640). GAO recommended that the ODNI, the Department of Homeland Security (DHS) and Department of Defense (DoD), take several actions to improve data quality and oversight related to the personnel security revocation process. As GAO notes, DHS and DoD have implemented security revocation processes in different ways which warrant additional ODNI oversight of agency revocation policies as well as collection of related metrics. We concur with GAO's formal recommendations for ODNI action.

The DNI, as Security Executive Agent, established the Security Executive Agent National Assessment Program (SNAP) in April 2014 to conduct oversight of personnel security processes across the Executive Branch. As a first step, the DNI has requested baseline data from agencies on personnel security clearance related processes. SNAP consists of annual agency self-assessments, on-site visits by the program office, and analysis of the data gathered. It complements the collection and analysis of security clearance performance metrics in place since 2008. Data gathered will be analyzed to establish standard processes as appropriate and to develop performance measures against these standards.

We have also enclosed technical comments on the draft GAO report from our National Counterintelligence Executive for your consideration. If you require additional information, please contact the Office of Legislative Affairs at (703) 275-2474.

Sincerely,

Deirdre M. Walsh
Director of Legislative Affairs

Enclosure

Appendix V: GAO Contact and Staff Acknowledgments

GAO Contact	Brenda S. Farrell, (202) 512-3604 or farrellb@gao.gov
Staff Acknowledgments	In addition to the contact named above, Margaret A. Best (Assistant Director), Renee S. Brown, Grace Coleman, Sara Cradic, Randy DeLeon, Cynthia Grant, Mary Jo LaCasse, Amie Lesser, David E. Moser, Kelly Rubin, and Michael Willems made major contributions to this report.

Related GAO Products

Personnel Security Clearances: Actions Needed to Ensure Quality of Background Investigations and Resulting Decisions. GAO-14-138T. Washington, D.C.: February 11, 2014.

Personnel Security Clearances: Actions Needed to Help Ensure Correct Designations of National Security Positions. GAO-14-139T. Washington, D.C.: November 20, 2013.

Personnel Security Clearances: Opportunities Exist to Improve Quality Throughout the Process. GAO-14-186T. Washington, D.C.: November 13, 2013.

Personnel Security Clearances: Full Development and Implementation of Metrics Needed to Measure Quality of Process. GAO-14-157T. Washington, D.C.: October 31, 2013.

Personnel Security Clearances: Further Actions Needed to Improve the Process and Realize Efficiencies. GAO-13-728T. Washington, D.C.: June 20, 2013.

Managing for Results: Agencies Should More Fully Develop Priority Goals under the GPRA Modernization Act. GAO-13-174. Washington, D.C.: April 19, 2013.

Security Clearances: Agencies Need Clearly Defined Policy for Determining Civilian Position Requirements. GAO-12-800. Washington, D.C.: July 12, 2012.

Personnel Security Clearances: Continuing Leadership and Attention Can Enhance Momentum Gained from Reform Effort. GAO-12-815T. Washington, D.C.: June 21, 2012.

2012 Annual Report: Opportunities to Reduce Duplication, Overlap and Fragmentation, Achieve Savings, and Enhance Revenue. GAO-12-342SP. Washington, D.C.: February 28, 2012.

Background Investigations: Office of Personnel Management Needs to Improve Transparency of Its Pricing and Seek Cost Savings. GAO-12-197. Washington, D.C.: February 28, 2012.

GAO's 2011 High-Risk Series: An Update. GAO-11-394T. Washington, D.C.: February 17, 2011.

High-Risk Series: An Update. GAO-11-278. Washington, D.C.: February 16, 2011.

Personnel Security Clearances: Overall Progress Has Been Made to Reform the Governmentwide Security Clearance Process. GAO-11-232T. Washington, D.C.: December 1, 2010.

Personnel Security Clearances: Progress Has Been Made to Improve Timeliness but Continued Oversight Is Needed to Sustain Momentum. GAO-11-65. Washington, D.C.: November 19, 2010.

DOD Personnel Clearances: Preliminary Observations on DOD's Progress on Addressing Timeliness and Quality Issues. GAO-11-185T. Washington, D.C.: November 16, 2010.

Personnel Security Clearances: An Outcome-Focused Strategy and Comprehensive Reporting of Timeliness and Quality Would Provide Greater Visibility over the Clearance Process. GAO-10-117T. Washington, D.C.: October 1, 2009.

Personnel Security Clearances: Progress Has Been Made to Reduce Delays but Further Actions Are Needed to Enhance Quality and Sustain Reform Efforts. GAO-09-684T. Washington, D.C.: September 15, 2009.

Personnel Security Clearances: An Outcome-Focused Strategy Is Needed to Guide Implementation of the Reformed Clearance Process. GAO-09-488. Washington, D.C.: May 19, 2009.

DOD Personnel Clearances: Comprehensive Timeliness Reporting, Complete Clearance Documentation, and Quality Measures Are Needed to Further Improve the Clearance Process. GAO-09-400. Washington, D.C.: May 19, 2009.

High-Risk Series: An Update. GAO-09-271. Washington, D.C.: January 2009.

Personnel Security Clearances: Preliminary Observations on Joint Reform Efforts to Improve the Government wide Clearance Eligibility Process. GAO-08-1050T. Washington, D.C.: July 30, 2008.

Personnel Clearances: Key Factors for Reforming the Security Clearance Process. GAO-08-776T. Washington, D.C.: May 22, 2008.

Employee Security: Implementation of Identification Cards and DOD's Personnel Security Clearance Program Need Improvement. GAO-08-551T. Washington, D.C.: April 9, 2008.

Personnel Clearances: Key Factors to Consider in Efforts to Reform Security Clearance Processes. GAO-08-352T. Washington, D.C.: February 27, 2008.

DOD Personnel Clearances: DOD Faces Multiple Challenges in Its Efforts to Improve Clearance Processes for Industry Personnel. GAO-08-470T. Washington, D.C.: February 13, 2008.

DOD Personnel Clearances: Improved Annual Reporting Would Enable More Informed Congressional Oversight. GAO-08-350. Washington, D.C.: February 13, 2008.

DOD Personnel Clearances: Delays and Inadequate Documentation Found for Industry Personnel. GAO-07-842T. Washington, D.C.: May 17, 2007.

High-Risk Series: An Update. GAO-07-310. Washington, D.C.: January 2007.

DOD Personnel Clearances: Additional OMB Actions Are Needed to Improve the Security Clearance Process. GAO-06-1070. Washington, D.C.: September 28, 2006.

DOD Personnel Clearances: New Concerns Slow Processing of Clearances for Industry Personnel. GAO-06-748T. Washington, D.C.: May 17, 2006.

DOD Personnel Clearances: Funding Challenges and Other Impediments Slow Clearances for Industry Personnel. GAO-06-747T. Washington, D.C.: May 17, 2006.

DOD Personnel Clearances: Government Plan Addresses Some Long-standing Problems with DOD's Program, But Concerns Remain. GAO-06-233T. Washington, D.C.: November 9, 2005.

DOD Personnel Clearances: Some Progress Has Been Made but Hurdles Remain to Overcome the Challenges That Led to GAO's High-Risk Designation. GAO-05-842T. Washington, D.C.: June 28, 2005.

High-Risk Series: An Update. GAO-05-207. Washington, D.C.: January 2005.

DOD Personnel Clearances: Preliminary Observations Related to Backlogs and Delays in Determining Security Clearance Eligibility for Industry Personnel. GAO-04-202T. Washington, D.C.: May 6, 2004.